AWS Direct Connect User Guide

A catalogue record for this book is available from the Hong Kong Public Libraries.

Published in Hong Kong by Samurai Media Limited.

Email: info@samuraimedia.org

ISBN 9789888407804

Contents

What is AWS Direct Connect?

AWS Direct Connect links your internal network to an AWS Direct Connect location over a standard 1-gigabit or 10-gigabit Ethernet fiber-optic cable. One end of the cable is connected to your router, the other to an AWS Direct Connect router. With this connection in place, you can create *virtual interfaces* directly to public AWS services (for example, to Amazon S3) or to Amazon VPC, bypassing Internet service providers in your network path. An AWS Direct Connect location provides access to AWS in the region with which it is associated, and you can use a single connection in a public region or AWS GovCloud (US) to access public AWS services in all other public regions.

The following diagram shows how AWS Direct Connect interfaces with your network.

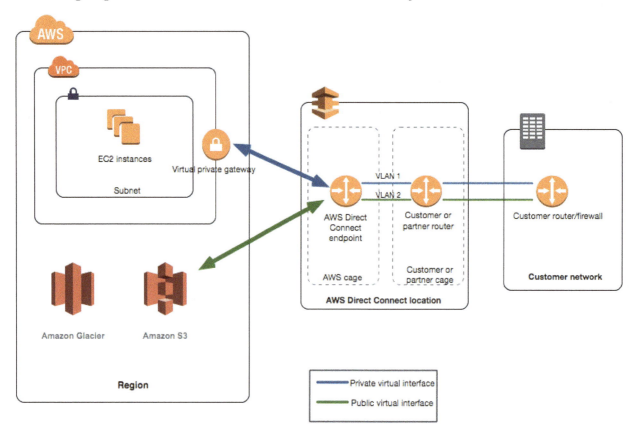

Topics

- AWS Direct Connect Components
- Network Requirements
- AWS Direct Connect Limits
- Resources
- Accessing a Remote AWS Region
- Routing Policies and BGP Communities

AWS Direct Connect Components

The following are the key components that you'll use for AWS Direct Connect.

Connection	Create a *connection* in an AWS Direct Connect location to establish a network connection from your premises to an AWS region. For more information, see Connections.
Virtual Interface	Create a *virtual interface* to enable access to AWS services. A public virtual interface enables access to public-facing services, such as Amazon S3. A private virtual interface enables access to your VPC. For more information, see Virtual Interfaces and Prerequisites for Virtual Interfaces.

Network Requirements

To use AWS Direct Connect in an AWS Direct Connect location, your network must meet one of the following conditions:

- Your network is colocated with an existing AWS Direct Connect location. For more information about available AWS Direct Connect locations, see AWS Direct Connect Product Details.
- You are working with an AWS Direct Connect partner who is a member of the AWS Partner Network (APN). For information, see APN Partners Supporting AWS Direct Connect.
- You are working with an independent service provider to connect to AWS Direct Connect.

In addition, your network must meet the following conditions:

- Your network must use single mode fiber with a 1000BASE-LX (1310nm) transceiver for 1 gigabit Ethernet, or a 10GBASE-LR (1310nm) transceiver for 10 gigabit Ethernet.
- Auto-negotiation for the port must be disabled. Port speed and full-duplex mode must be configured manually.
- 802.1Q VLAN encapsulation must be supported across the entire connection, including intermediate devices.
- Your device must support Border Gateway Protocol (BGP) and BGP MD5 authentication.
- (Optional) You can configure Bidirectional Forwarding Detection (BFD) on your network. Asynchronous BFD is automatically enabled for AWS Direct Connect virtual interfaces, but will not take effect until you configure it on your router.

AWS Direct Connect supports both the IPv4 and IPv6 communication protocols. IPv6 addresses provided by public AWS services are accessible through AWS Direct Connect public virtual interfaces.

AWS Direct Connect supports a maximum transmission unit (MTU) of up to 1522 bytes at the physical connection layer (14 bytes ethernet header + 4 bytes VLAN tag + 1500 bytes IP datagram + 4 bytes FCS).

AWS Direct Connect Limits

The following table lists the limits related to AWS Direct Connect. Unless indicated otherwise, you can request an increase for any of these limits by using the AWS Direct Connect Limits form.

Component	Limit	Comments
Virtual interfaces per AWS Direct Connect connection	50	This limit cannot be increased.
Active AWS Direct Connect connections per region per account	10	This limit can be increased upon request.

Component	Limit	Comments
Routes per Border Gateway Protocol (BGP) session on a private virtual interface	100	This limit cannot be increased.
Routes per Border Gateway Protocol (BGP) session on a public virtual interface	1,000	This limit cannot be increased.
Number of connections per link aggregation group (LAG)	4	This limit can be increased upon request.
Number of link aggregation groups (LAGs) per region	10	This limit can be increased upon request.
Number of Direct Connect gateways per account	200	This limit can be increased upon request.
Virtual private gateways per Direct Connect gateway	10	This limit cannot be increased.
Virtual interfaces per Direct Connect gateway	30	This limit can be increased upon request.

Resources

The following related resources can help you as you work with this service.

Resource	Description
AWS Direct Connect product information	General product overview.
Pricing	Calculate monthly costs.
AWS Developer Tools	Links to developer tools, SDKs, IDE toolkits, and command line tools for developing and managing AWS applications.
AWS Direct Connect FAQ	The top questions asked about this product.
AWS Direct Connect Forum	A community-based forum for discussing technical questions related to AWS Direct Connect.
AWS Support Center	The hub for creating and managing your AWS Support cases. Also includes links to other helpful resources, such as forums, technical FAQs, service health status, and AWS Trusted Advisor.
Contact Us	A central contact point for inquiries concerning AWS billing, account, events, abuse, and other issues.

Accessing a Remote AWS Region

AWS Direct Connect locations in public regions or AWS GovCloud (US) can access public services in any other public region (excluding China (Beijing)). In addition, AWS Direct Connect connections in public regions or AWS GovCloud (US) can be configured to access a VPC in your account in any other public region (excluding China (Beijing)). You can therefore use a single AWS Direct Connect connection to build multi-region services. All networking traffic remains on the AWS global network backbone, regardless of whether you access public AWS services or a VPC in another region.

Any data transfer out of a remote region is billed at the remote region data transfer rate. For more information about data transfer pricing, see the Pricing section on the AWS Direct Connect detail page.

For more information about the routing polices and supported BGP communities for an AWS Direct Connect connection, see Routing Policies and BGP Communities.

Accessing Public Services in a Remote Region

To access public resources in a remote region, you must set up a public virtual interface and establish a Border Gateway Protocol (BGP) session. For more information, see Virtual Interfaces.

After you have created a public virtual interface and established a BGP session to it, your router learns the routes of the other public AWS regions. For more information about prefixes currently advertised by AWS, see AWS IP Address Ranges in the *Amazon Web Services General Reference.*

Accessing VPCs in a Remote Region

You can create a *Direct Connect gateway* in any public region and use it to connect your AWS Direct Connect connection over a private virtual interface to VPCs in your account that are located in different regions. For more information, see Direct Connect Gateways.

Alternatively, you can create a public virtual interface for your AWS Direct Connect connection and then establish a VPN connection to your VPC in the remote region. For more information about configuring VPN connectivity to a VPC, see Scenarios for Using Amazon Virtual Private Cloud in the *Amazon VPC User Guide.*

Routing Policies and BGP Communities

AWS Direct Connect applies inbound and outbound routing policies for a public AWS Direct Connect connection. You can also make use of Border Gateway Protocol (BGP) community tags on advertised Amazon routes and apply BGP community tags on the routes you advertise to Amazon.

Routing Policies

If you're using AWS Direct Connect to access public AWS services, you must specify the public IPv4 prefixes or IPv6 prefixes to advertise over BGP.

The following inbound routing policies apply:

- You must own the public prefixes and they must be registered as such in the appropriate regional internet registry.
- Traffic must be destined to Amazon public prefixes. Transitive routing between connections is not supported.
- AWS Direct Connect performs inbound packet filtering to validate that the source of the traffic originated from your advertised prefix.

The following outbound routing policies apply:

- AS_PATH is used to determine the routing path, and AWS Direct Connect is the preferred path for traffic sourced from Amazon. Only public ASNs are used internally for route selection.
- AWS Direct Connect advertises all local and remote AWS Region prefixes where available and includes on-net prefixes from other AWS non-region points of presence (PoP) where available; for example, CloudFront and Route 53.
- AWS Direct Connect advertises prefixes with a minimum path length of 3.
- AWS Direct Connect advertises all public prefixes with the well-known NO_EXPORT BGP community.
- If you have multiple AWS Direct Connect connections, you can adjust the load-sharing of inbound traffic by advertising prefixes with similar path attributes.
- The prefixes advertised by AWS Direct Connect must not be advertised beyond the network boundaries of your connection; for example, these prefixes must not be included in any public internet routing table.

BGP Communities

AWS Direct Connect supports a range of BGP community tags to help control the scope (regional or global) and route preference of traffic.

Scope BGP Communities

You can apply BGP community tags on the public prefixes you advertise to Amazon to indicate how far to propagate your prefixes in the Amazon network—for the local AWS Region only, all regions within a continent, or all public regions.

You can use the following BGP communities for your prefixes:

- 7224:9100—Local AWS Region
- 7224:9200—All AWS regions for a continent (for example, North America–wide)
- 7224:9300—Global (all public AWS Regions)

Note
If you do not apply any community tags, prefixes are advertised to all public AWS regions (global) by default.

The communities 7224:1 – 7224:65535 are reserved by AWS Direct Connect.

In addition, the well-known `NO_EXPORT` BGP community is supported for both public and private virtual interfaces.

AWS Direct Connect also provides BGP community tags on advertised Amazon routes. If you're using AWS Direct Connect to access public AWS services, this enables you to create filters based on these community tags.

AWS Direct Connect applies the following BGP communities to its advertised routes:

- `7224:8100`—Routes that originate from the same AWS Region in which the AWS Direct Connect point of presence is associated.
- `7224:8200`—Routes that originate from the same continent with which the AWS Direct Connect point of presence is associated.
- No tag—Global (all public AWS Regions).

Communities that are not supported for an AWS Direct Connect public connection are removed.

Local Preference BGP Communities

You can use local preference BGP community tags to achieve load balancing and route preference for incoming traffic to your network. For each prefix that you advertise over a BGP session, you can apply a community tag to indicate the priority of the associated path for returning traffic. Local preference BGP community tags are supported for private virtual interfaces.

The following local preference BGP community tags are supported:

- `7224:7100`—Low preference
- `7224:7200`—Medium preference
- `7224:7300`—High preference

Local preference BGP community tags are mutually exclusive. To load balance traffic across multiple AWS Direct Connect connections, apply the same community tag across the prefixes for the connections. To support failover across multiple AWS Direct Connect connections, apply a community tag with a higher preference to the prefixes for the primary or active virtual interface.

Local preference BGP community tags are evaluated before any AS_PATH attribute, and are evaluated in order from lowest to highest preference (where highest preference is preferred).

Getting Started with AWS Direct Connect

AWS Direct Connect enables you to directly interface your on-premises network with a device at an AWS Direct Connect location. The following procedures demonstrate the common scenarios to get set up with an AWS Direct Connect connection. You can also refer to the article How do I provision an AWS Direct Connect connection? in the Knowledge Center.

You can set up an AWS Direct Connect connection in one of the following ways.

Port speed	Method
1 Gbps or higher	Connect directly to an AWS device from your router at an AWS Direct Connect location.
1 Gbps or higher	Work with a partner in the AWS Partner Network (APN) or a network provider that will help you connect a router from your data center, office, or colocation environment to an AWS Direct Connect location. The network provider does not have to be a member of the APN to connect you.
Sub-1 Gbps	Work with a partner in the AWS Partner Network (APN) who will create a hosted connection for you. Sign up for AWS, and then follow the instructions to accept your hosted connection.

Topics

- Prerequisites
- Step 1: Sign Up for AWS
- Step 2: Request an AWS Direct Connect Connection
- Step 3: Download the LOA-CFA
- Step 4: Create a Virtual Interface
- Step 5: Download the Router Configuration
- Step 6: Verify Your Virtual Interface
- (Optional) Configure Redundant Connections

Prerequisites

For connections to AWS Direct Connect with port speeds of 1 Gbps or higher, ensure that your network meets the following requirements.

- Your network must use single mode fiber with a 1000BASE-LX (1310nm) transceiver for 1 gigabit Ethernet, or a 10GBASE-LR (1310nm) transceiver for 10 gigabit Ethernet.
- Auto-negotiation for the port must be disabled. Port speed and full-duplex mode must be configured manually.
- 802.1Q VLAN encapsulation must be supported across the entire connection, including intermediate devices.
- Your device must support Border Gateway Protocol (BGP) and BGP MD5 authentication.
- (Optional) You can configure Bidirectional Forwarding Detection (BFD) on your network. Asynchronous BFD is automatically enabled for AWS Direct Connect virtual interfaces, but will not take effect until you configure it on your router.

Step 1: Sign Up for AWS

To use AWS Direct Connect, you need an AWS account if you don't already have one.

To sign up for an AWS account

1. Open https://aws.amazon.com/, and then choose **Create an AWS Account**. **Note**
   This might be unavailable in your browser if you previously signed into the AWS Management Console. In that case, choose **Sign in to a different account**, and then choose **Create a new AWS account**.

2. Follow the online instructions.

   Part of the sign-up procedure involves receiving a phone call and entering a PIN using the phone keypad.

Step 2: Request an AWS Direct Connect Connection

For connections of 1 Gbps or higher, you can submit a connection request using the AWS Direct Connect console. Ensure that you have the following information:

- The port speed that you require: 1 Gbps or 10 Gbps. You cannot change the port speed after you've created the connection request.
- The AWS Direct Connect location at which the connection will be terminated.

If you require a port speed less than 1 Gbps, you cannot request a connection using the console. Instead, contact an APN partner, who will create a hosted connection for you, which you then accept. Skip the following procedure and go to (Sub-1 Gbps Only) Accept Your Hosted Connection.

To create a new AWS Direct Connect connection

1. Open the AWS Direct Connect console at https://console.aws.amazon.com/directconnect/.

2. In the navigation bar, select the region in which to connect to AWS Direct Connect. For more information, see AWS Regions and Endpoints.

3. On the **Welcome to AWS Direct Connect** screen, choose **Get Started with Direct Connect**.

4. In the **Create a Connection** dialog box, do the following:

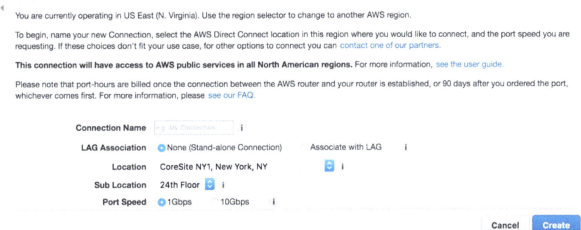

1. For **Connection Name**, enter a name for the connection.

2. For **LAG Association**, specify whether the connection is standalone, or if it should be associated with a link aggregation group (LAG) in your account. This option is only available if you have a LAG in your account. To associate the connection with a LAG, select the LAG ID. The connection is

13

created with the same port speed and location as specified in the LAG. For more information, see Link Aggregation Groups.

3. For **Location**, select the appropriate AWS Direct Connect location.

4. If applicable, for **Sub Location**, choose the floor closest to you or your network provider. This option is only available if the location has meet-me rooms (MMRs) in multiple floors of the building.

5. Select the appropriate port speed, and then choose **Create**.

   Your connection is listed on the **Connections** pane of the AWS Direct Connect console.

It can take up to 72 hours for AWS to review your request and provision a port for your connection. During this time, you may receive an email with a request for more information about your use case or the specified location. The email is sent to the email address that you used when you signed up for AWS. You must respond within 7 days or the connection is deleted.

For more information about creating and working with AWS Direct Connect connections, see Connections.

(Sub-1 Gbps Only) Accept Your Hosted Connection

If you requested a sub-1G connection from your selected partner, they create a hosted connection for you (you cannot create it yourself). You must accept it in the AWS Direct Connect console before you can create a virtual interface.

To accept a hosted connection

1. Open the AWS Direct Connect console at https://console.aws.amazon.com/directconnect/.

2. If necessary, select the region in which the hosted connection resides. For more information, see AWS Regions and Endpoints.

3. In the navigation pane, choose **Connections**.

4. In the **Connections** pane, select the hosted connection.

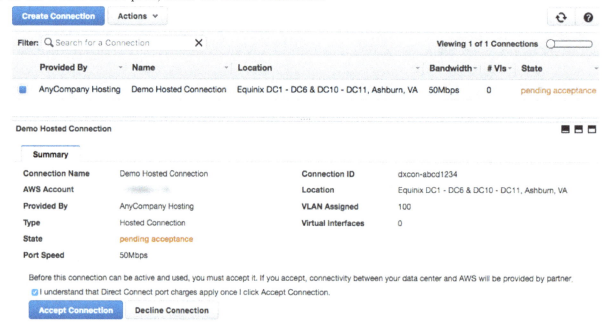

5. Select **I understand that Direct Connect port charges apply once I click Accept Connection**, and then choose **Accept Connection**.

6. Go to Step 4 to continue setting up your AWS Direct Connect connection.

14

Step 3: Download the LOA-CFA

After you request a connection, AWS makes a Letter of Authorization and Connecting Facility Assignment (LOA-CFA) available to you to download, or emails you with a request for more information. The LOA-CFA is the authorization to connect to AWS, and is required by the colocation provider or your network provider to establish the cross-network connection (cross-connect).

To download the LOA-CFA

1. Open the AWS Direct Connect console at https://console.aws.amazon.com/directconnect/.

2. In the navigation pane, choose **Connections** and select your connection.

3. Choose **Actions**, **Download LOA-CFA**. **Note**
   If the link is not enabled, the LOA-CFA is not yet available for you to download. Check your email for a request for more information. If it's still unavailable, or you haven't received an email after 72 hours, contact AWS Support.

4. Optionally enter the name of your provider to have it to appear with your company name as the requester in the LOA-CFA. Choose **Download**. The LOA-CFA is downloaded to your computer as a PDF file.

5. After you've downloaded the LOA-CFA, do one of the following:

   - If you're working with an APN member or network provider, send them the LOA-CFA so that they can order a cross-connect for you at the AWS Direct Connect location. If they cannot order the cross-connect for you, you can contact the colocation provider directly.
   - If you have equipment at the AWS Direct Connect location, contact the colocation provider to request a cross-network connection. You must be a customer of the colocation provider, and you must present them with the LOA-CFA that authorizes the connection to the AWS router, as well as the necessary information to connect to your network.

AWS Direct Connect locations that are listed as multiple sites (for example, Equinix DC1-DC6 & DC10-DC11) are set up as a campus. If your or your network provider's equipment is located in any of these sites, you will be able to request a cross connect to your assigned port even if it resides in a different building on the campus.

Important
A campus is treated as a single AWS Direct Connect location. To achieve high availability, configure connections to different AWS Direct Connect locations.

If you or your network partner experience issues establishing a physical connection, see Troubleshooting Layer 1 (Physical) Issues.

Step 4: Create a Virtual Interface

To begin using your AWS Direct Connect connection, you must create a virtual interface. You can create a private virtual interface to connect to your VPC, or you can create a public virtual interface to connect to public AWS services that aren't in a VPC. When you create a private virtual interface to a VPC, you need a private virtual interface for each VPC to which to connect. For example, you need three private virtual interfaces to connect to three VPCs.

Before you begin, ensure that you have the following information:

- **Connection**: The AWS Direct Connect connection or link aggregation group (LAG) for which you are creating the virtual interface.
- **Virtual interface name**: A name for the virtual interface.
- **Virtual interface owner**: If you're creating the virtual interface for another account, you need the AWS account ID of the other account.
- (Private virtual interface only) **Connection to**: For connecting to a VPC in the same region, you need the virtual private gateway for your VPC. The ASN for the Amazon side of the BGP session is inherited from the virtual private gateway. When you create a virtual private gateway, you can specify your own

private ASN. Otherwise, Amazon provides a default ASN. For more information, see Create a Virtual Private Gateway in the *Amazon VPC User Guide*. For connecting to a VPC through a Direct Connect gateway, you need the Direct Connect gateway. For more information, see Direct Connect Gateways.

- **VLAN**: A unique virtual local area network (VLAN) tag that's not already in use on your connection. The value must be between 1 and 4094 and must comply with the Ethernet 802.1Q standard. This tag is required for any traffic traversing the AWS Direct Connect connection.
- **Address family**: Whether the BGP peering session will be over IPv4 or IPv6.
- **Peer IP addresses**: A virtual interface can support a BGP peering session for IPv4, IPv6, or one of each (dual-stack). You cannot create multiple BGP sessions for the same IP addressing family on the same virtual interface. The IP address ranges are assigned to each end of the virtual interface for the BGP peering session.
  - IPv4:
    - (Public virtual interface only) You must specify unique public IPv4 addresses (/30) that you own.
    - (Private virtual interface only) Amazon can generate private IPv4 addresses for you. If you specify your own, ensure that you specify private CIDRs for your router interface and the AWS Direct Connect interface only (for example, do not specify other IP addresses from your local network).
  - IPv6: Amazon automatically allocates you a /125 IPv6 CIDR. You cannot specify your own peer IPv6 addresses.
- **BGP information**:
  - A public or private Border Gateway Protocol (BGP) Autonomous System Number (ASN) for your side of the BGP session. If you are using a public ASN, you must own it. If you are using a private ASN, it must be in the 64512 to 65535 range. Autonomous System (AS) prepending does not work if you use a private ASN for a public virtual interface.
  - An MD5 BGP authentication key. You can provide your own, or you can let Amazon generate one for you.
- (Public virtual interface only) **Prefixes you want to advertise**: Public IPv4 routes or IPv6 routes to advertise over BGP. You must advertise at least one prefix using BGP, up to a maximum of 1,000 prefixes.
  - IPv4: The IPv4 CIDR must not overlap with another public IPv4 CIDR announced via AWS Direct Connect. If you do not own public IPv4 addresses, your network provider might be able to provide you with a public IPv4 CIDR. If not, contact AWS Support to request a /31 public IPv4 CIDR (and provide a use case in your request).
  - IPv6: Specify a prefix length of /64 or shorter.

To provision a public virtual interface to non-VPC services

1. Open the AWS Direct Connect console at https://console.aws.amazon.com/directconnect/.

2. In the navigation pane, choose **Connections**, select the connection to use, and then choose **Actions**, **Create Virtual Interface**.

3. In the **Create a Virtual Interface** pane, choose **Public**.

Create a Virtual Interface

You may choose to create a private or public virtual interface. Select the appropriate option below.
   Private - A private virtual interface should be used to access an Amazon VPC using private IP addresses.
○ Public - A public virtual interface can access all AWS public services (including EC2, S3, and DynamoDB) using public IP addresses.

Define Your New Public Virtual Interface

This virtual interface will have access to AWS public services in all US regions. For more information, see the user guide.

Enter the name of your virtual interface. If youre creating a virtual interface for another account, youll need to provide the other AWS account ID. For more information about virtual interface ownership, see 'Hosted Virtual Interfaces' in the AWS Direct Connect Getting Started Guide.

Connection:	dxcon-fgvg1fy7 (USWest1) ⬍ ℹ
Virtual Interface Name:	ℹ
Virtual Interface Owner:	○ My AWS Account ○ Another AWS Account ℹ

Enter the VLAN ID, if not already supplied by your AWS Direct Connect partner, and the IP Addresses for your router interface and the AWS Direct Connect interface.

VLAN:	ℹ
Address family:	○ IPv4 ○ IPv6 ℹ
Your router peer IP:	ℹ
Amazon router peer IP:	ℹ

Before you can use your virtual interface, we must establish a BGP session. You must provide an ASN for your router and any prefixes you would like to announce to AWS. You will also need an MD5 key to authenticate the BGP session. We can generate one for you, or you can supply your own.

BGP ASN:	ℹ
Auto-generate BGP key:	☑ ℹ
Prefixes you want to advertise:	ℹ

It may take up to 72 hours to verify that your IP prefixes are valid for use with Direct Connect.

4. In the **Define Your New Public Virtual Interface** dialog box, do the following and choose **Continue**:

   1. For **Connection**, select an existing physical connection on which to create the virtual interface.

   2. For **Virtual Interface Name**, enter a name for the virtual interface.

   3. For **Virtual Interface Owner**, select the **My AWS Account** option if the virtual interface is for your AWS account.

   4. For **VLAN**, enter the ID number for your virtual local area network (VLAN).

   5. If you're configuring an IPv4 BGP peer, choose **IPv4**, and do the following:

      - For **Your router peer IP**, enter the IPv4 CIDR destination address to which Amazon should send traffic.
      - For **Amazon router peer IP**, enter the IPv4 CIDR address to use to send traffic to Amazon.

   6. If you're configuring an IPv6 BGP peer, choose **IPv6**. The peer IPv6 addresses are automatically assigned from Amazon's pool of IPv6 addresses. You cannot specify custom IPv6 addresses.

   7. For **BGP ASN**, enter the Border Gateway Protocol (BGP) Autonomous System Number (ASN) of your gateway.

   8. To have AWS generate a BGP key, select the **Auto-generate BGP key** check box.

      To provide your own BGP key, clear the **Auto-generate BGP key** check box. For **BGP Authentication Key**, enter your BGP MD5 key.

   9. For **Prefixes you want to advertise**, enter the IPv4 CIDR destination addresses (separated by commas) to which traffic should be routed over the virtual interface.

5. Download your router configuration. For more information, see Step 5: Download the Router Configuration.

Note

AWS requests additional information from you if your public prefixes or ASNs belong to an ISP or network carrier. This can be a document using an official company letterhead or an email from the company's domain name verifying that the network prefix/ASN may be used by you.

When you create a public virtual interface, it can take up to 72 hours for AWS to review and approve your request.

To provision a private virtual interface to a VPC

1. Open the AWS Direct Connect console at https://console.aws.amazon.com/directconnect/.

2. In the navigation pane, choose **Connections**, select the connection to use, and choose **Actions**, **Create Virtual Interface**.

3. In the **Create a Virtual Interface** pane, select **Private**.

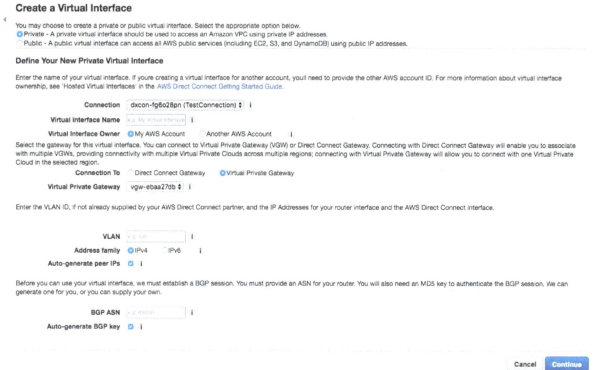

4. Under **Define Your New Private Virtual Interface**, do the following and choose **Continue**:

    1. For **Virtual Interface Name**, enter a name for the virtual interface.

    2. For **Virtual Interface Owner**, select the **My AWS Account** option if the virtual interface is for your AWS account.

    3. For **Connection To**, choose **Virtual Private Gateway** and select the virtual private gateway to which to connect.

    4. For **VLAN**, enter the ID number for your virtual local area network (VLAN).

    5. If you're configuring an IPv4 BGP peer, choose **IPv4**, and do the following:
        - To have AWS generate your router IP address and Amazon IP address, select **Auto-generate peer IPs**.
        - To specify these IP addresses yourself, clear the **Auto-generate peer IPs** check box. For **Your router peer IP**, enter the destination IPv4 CIDR address to which Amazon should send traffic. For **Amazon router peer IP**, enter the IPv4 CIDR address to use to send traffic to AWS.

    6. If you're configuring an IPv6 BGP peer, choose **IPv6**. The peer IPv6 addresses are automatically assigned from Amazon's pool of IPv6 addresses. You cannot specify custom IPv6 addresses.

    7. For **BGP ASN**, enter the Border Gateway Protocol (BGP) Autonomous System Number (ASN) of your gateway.

8. To have AWS generate a BGP key, select the **Auto-generate BGP key** check box.

   To provide your own BGP key, clear the **Auto-generate BGP key** check box. For **BGP Authentication Key**, enter your BGP MD5 key.

5. Download your router configuration. For more information, see Step 5: Download the Router Configuration.

Note

If you use the VPC wizard to create a VPC, route propagation is automatically enabled for you. With route propagation, routes are automatically populated to the route tables in your VPC. If you choose, you can disable route propagation. For more information, see Enable Route Propagation in Your Route Table in the *Amazon VPC User Guide.*

Step 5: Download the Router Configuration

After you have created a virtual interface for your AWS Direct Connect connection, you can download the router configuration file. The file contains the necessary commands to configure your router for use with your private or public virtual interface.

To download a router configuration

1. Open the AWS Direct Connect console at https://console.aws.amazon.com/directconnect/.

2. In the **Virtual Interfaces** pane, select the virtual interface and then choose **Actions, Download Router Configuration**.

3. In the **Download Router Configuration** dialog box, do the following:

   1. For **Vendor**, select the manufacturer of your router.

   2. For **Platform**, select the model of your router.

   3. For **Software**, select the software version for your router.

4. Choose **Download**, and then use the appropriate configuration for your router to ensure that you can connect to AWS Direct Connect.

For example configuration files, see Example Router Configuration Files.

After you configure your router, the status of the virtual interface goes to UP. If the virtual interface remains down and you cannot ping the AWS Direct Connect device's peer IP address, see Troubleshooting Layer 2 (Data Link) Issues. If you can ping the peer IP address, see Troubleshooting Layer 3/4 (Network/Transport) Issues. If the BGP peering session is established but you cannot route traffic, see Troubleshooting Routing Issues.

Step 6: Verify Your Virtual Interface

After you have established virtual interfaces to the AWS Cloud or to Amazon VPC, you can verify your AWS Direct Connect connection using the following procedures.

To verify your virtual interface connection to the AWS Cloud

- Run `traceroute` and verify that the AWS Direct Connect identifier is in the network trace.

To verify your virtual interface connection to Amazon VPC

1. Using a pingable AMI, such as an Amazon Linux AMI, launch an EC2 instance into the VPC that is attached to your virtual private gateway. The Amazon Linux AMIs are available in the **Quick Start** tab when you use the instance launch wizard in the Amazon EC2 console. For more information, see Launch an Instance in the *Amazon EC2 User Guide for Linux Instances*. Ensure that the security group that's associated with the instance includes a rule permitting inbound ICMP traffic (for the ping request).

2. After the instance is running, get its private IPv4 address (for example, 10.0.0.4). The Amazon EC2 console displays the address as part of the instance details.

3. Ping the private IPv4 address and get a response.

(Optional) Configure Redundant Connections

To provide for failover, we recommend that you request and configure two dedicated connections to AWS, as shown in the following figure. These connections can terminate on one or two routers in your network.

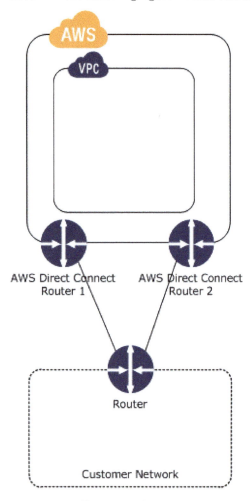

There are different configuration choices available when you provision two dedicated connections:

- Active/Active (BGP multipath). This is the default configuration, where both connections are active. AWS Direct Connect supports multipathing to multiple virtual interfaces within the same location, and traffic is load-shared between interfaces based on flow. If one connection becomes unavailable, all traffic is routed through the other connection.
- Active/Passive (failover). One connection is handling traffic, and the other is on standby. If the active connection becomes unavailable, all traffic is routed through the passive connection. You need to prepend the AS path to the routes on one of your links for that to be the passive link.

How you configure the connections doesn't affect redundancy, but it does affect the policies that determine how your data is routed over both connections. We recommend that you configure both connections as active.

If you use a VPN connection for redundancy, ensure that you implement a health check and failover mechanism, and check your route table routing.

To achieve high availability, we strongly recommend that you configure connections to different AWS Direct Connect locations. For more information about high availability options, see Multiple Data Center HA Network Connectivity.

Connections

To create an AWS Direct Connect connection, you need the following information:

- **AWS Direct Connect location**

  Work with a partner in the AWS Partner Network (APN) to help you establish network circuits between an AWS Direct Connect location and your data center, office, or colocation environment, or to provide colocation space within the same facility as the AWS Direct Connect location. For the list of AWS Direct Connect partners who belong to the APN, see APN Partners Supporting AWS Direct Connect.

- **Port speed**

  AWS Direct Connect supports two port speeds: 1 Gbps: 1000BASE-LX (1310nm) over single-mode fiber and 10 Gbps: 10GBASE-LR (1310nm) over single-mode fiber. You cannot change the port speed after you've created the connection request. If you need to change the port speed, you must create and configure a new connection.

  For port speeds less than 1 Gbps, you cannot request a connection using the console. Instead, you can contact an APN partner who supports AWS Direct Connect and who can provision a hosted connection for you.

After you've requested the connection, AWS makes a Letter of Authorization and Connecting Facility Assignment (LOA-CFA) available to you to download, or emails you with a request for more information. If you receive a request for more information, you must respond within 7 days or the connection is deleted. The LOA-CFA is the authorization to connect to AWS, and is required by your network provider to order a cross connect for you. You cannot order a cross connect for yourself in the AWS Direct Connect location if you do not have equipment there; your network provider does this for you.

For information about associating a connection with a link aggregation group (LAG), see Associating a Connection with a LAG.

After you've created a connection, create a virtual interface to connect to public and private AWS resources. For more information, see Virtual Interfaces.

Topics

- Creating a Connection
- Viewing Connection Details
- Deleting a Connection
- Accepting a Hosted Connection

Creating a Connection

You can create a standalone connection, or you can create a connection to associate with a LAG in your account. If you associate a connection with a LAG, it's created with the same port speed and location as specified in the LAG.

If you do not have equipment at an AWS Direct Connect location, first contact an AWS partner at the AWS Partner Network (APN). For more information, see APN Partners Supporting AWS Direct Connect.

To create a new connection

1. Open the AWS Direct Connect console at https://console.aws.amazon.com/directconnect/.

2. In the navigation bar, select the region in which to connect to AWS Direct Connect. For more information, see AWS Regions and Endpoints.

3. In the navigation pane, choose **Connections**, **Create Connection**.

4. In the **Create a Connection** dialog box, enter the following values, and then choose **Create**:

   Create a Connection

   You are currently operating in US East (N. Virginia). Use the region selector to change to another AWS region.

   To begin, name your new Connection, select the AWS Direct Connect location in this region where you would like to connect, and the port speed you are requesting. If these choices don't fit your use case, for other options to connect you can contact one of our partners.

   This connection will have access to AWS public services in all North American regions. For more information, see the user guide.

   Please note that port-hours are billed once the connection between the AWS router and your router is established, or 90 days after you ordered the port, whichever comes first. For more information, please see our FAQ.

Connection Name	e.g. My Connection
LAG Association	○ None (Stand-alone Connection) Associate with LAG
Location	CoreSite NY1, New York, NY
Sub Location	24th Floor
Port Speed	○ 1Gbps 10Gbps

   Cancel   Create

   1. For **Connection Name**, enter a name for the connection.

   2. For **LAG Association**, specify whether the connection is standalone, or if it should be associated with a LAG. If you associate the connection with a LAG, select the LAG ID.

   3. For **Location**, select the appropriate AWS Direct Connect location.

   4. If applicable, for **Sub Location**, choose the floor closest to you or your network provider. This option is only available if the location has meet-me rooms (MMRs) in multiple floors of the building.

   5. Select the appropriate port speed that is compatible with your existing network.

To create a connection using the command line or API

- create-connection (AWS CLI)
- CreateConnection (AWS Direct Connect API)

Downloading the LOA-CFA

After AWS has processed your connection request, you can download the Letter of Authorization and Connecting Facility Assignment (LOA-CFA).

To download the LOA-CFA

1. Open the AWS Direct Connect console at https://console.aws.amazon.com/directconnect/.

2. In the navigation pane, choose **Connections**.

3. Choose **Actions, Download LOA-CFA**. **Note**
   If the link is not enabled, the LOA-CFA is not yet available for you to download. Check your email for a request for more information. If it's still unavailable, or you haven't received an email after 72 hours, contact AWS Support.

4. In the dialog box, optionally enter the name of your provider to have it appear with your company name as the requester in the LOA-CFA. Choose **Download**. The LOA-CFA is downloaded to your computer as a PDF file.

5. Send the LOA-CFA to your network provider or colocation provider so that they can order a cross connect for you. The contact process can vary for each colocation provider. For more information, see Requesting Cross Connects at AWS Direct Connect Locations.

The LOA-CFA expires after 90 days. If your connection is not up after 90 days, we send you an email alerting you that the LOA-CFA has expired. To refresh the LOA-CFA with a new issue date, download it again from the AWS Direct Connect console. If you do not take any action, we delete the connection.

Note
Port-hour billing starts 90 days after you created the connection, or after the connection between your router and the AWS Direct Connect endpoint is established, whichever comes first. For more information, see AWS Direct Connect Pricing. If you no longer want the connection after you've reissued the LOA-CFA, you must delete the connection yourself. For more information, see Deleting a Connection.

To download the LOA-CFA using the command line or API

- describe-loa (AWS CLI)
- DescribeLoa (AWS Direct Connect API)

Viewing Connection Details

You can view the current status of your connection. You can also view your connection ID (for example, `dxcon-12nikabc`) and verify that it matches the connection ID on the Letter of Authorization and Connecting Facility Assignment (LOA-CFA) that you received or downloaded.

To view details about a connection

1. Open the AWS Direct Connect console at https://console.aws.amazon.com/directconnect/.

2. If necessary, change the region in the navigation bar. For more information, see Regions and Endpoints.

3. In the navigation pane, choose **Connections**.

4. In the **Connections** pane, select a connection to view its details.

   The service provider associated with the connection is listed in the **Provided By** column.

To describe a connection using the command line or API

- describe-connections (AWS CLI)
- DescribeConnections (AWS Direct Connect API)

Deleting a Connection

You can delete a connection as long as there are no virtual interfaces attached to it. Deleting your connection stops all port hour charges for this connection. AWS Direct Connect data transfer charges are associated with virtual interfaces. Any cross connect or network circuit charges are independent of AWS Direct Connect and must be cancelled separately. For more information about how to delete a virtual interface, see Deleting a Virtual Interface.

If the connection is part of a link aggregation group (LAG), you cannot delete the connection if doing so will cause the LAG to fall below its setting for minimum number of operational connections.

To delete a connection

1. Open the AWS Direct Connect console at https://console.aws.amazon.com/directconnect/.

2. If necessary, change the region in the navigation bar. For more information, see Regions and Endpoints.

3. In the navigation pane, choose **Connections**.

4. In the **Connections** pane, select the connection to delete, and then choose **Actions, Delete Connection**.

5. In the **Delete Connection** dialog box, choose **Delete**.

To delete a connection using the command line or API

- delete-connection (AWS CLI)
- DeleteConnection (AWS Direct Connect API)

Accepting a Hosted Connection

If you are interested in purchasing a hosted connection, you must contact a partner in the AWS Partner Network (APN). The partner provisions the connection for you. After the connection is configured, it appears in the **Connections** pane in the AWS Direct Connect console.

Before you can begin using a hosted connection, you must accept the connection.

To accept a hosted connection

1. Open the AWS Direct Connect console at https://console.aws.amazon.com/directconnect/.

2. If necessary, change the region in the navigation bar. For more information, see Regions and Endpoints.

3. In the navigation pane, choose **Connections**.

4. In the **Connections** pane, select a connection.

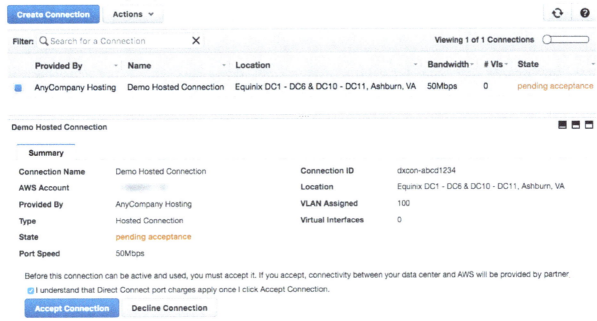

5. Select **I understand that Direct Connect port charges apply once I click Accept Connection**, and then choose **Accept Connection**.

To accept a hosted connection using the command line or API

- confirm-connection (AWS CLI)
- ConfirmConnection (AWS Direct Connect API)

Requesting Cross Connects at AWS Direct Connect Locations

After you have downloaded your Letter of Authorization and Connecting Facility Assignment (LOA-CFA), you need to complete your cross-network connection, also known as a *cross connect*. If you already have equipment located in an AWS Direct Connect location, contact the appropriate provider to complete the cross connect. For specific instructions for each provider, see the table below. Contact your provider for cross connect pricing. After the cross connect is established, you can create the virtual interfaces using the AWS Direct Connect console.

Some locations are set up as a campus. For more information, see AWS Direct Connect Locations.

If you do not already have equipment located in an AWS Direct Connect location, you can work with one of the partners in the AWS Partner Network (APN) to help you to connect to an AWS Direct Connect location. For a list of partners in the APN with experience connecting to AWS Direct Connect, see APN Partners supporting AWS Direct Connect. You need to share the LOA-CFA with your selected provider to facilitate your cross connect request.

An AWS Direct Connect connection can provide access to resources in other regions. For more information, see Accessing a Remote AWS Region.

Note
If the cross connect is not completed within 90 days, the authority granted by the LOA-CFA expires. To renew a LOA-CFA that has expired, you can download it again from the AWS Direct Connect console. For more information, see Downloading the LOA-CFA.

- Asia Pacific (Tokyo)
- Asia Pacific (Seoul)
- Asia Pacific (Singapore)
- Asia Pacific (Sydney)
- Asia Pacific (Mumbai)
- Canada (Central)
- China (Beijing)
- EU (Frankfurt)
- EU (Ireland)
- EU (London)
- EU (Paris)
- South America (São Paulo)
- US East (N. Virginia)
- US East (Ohio)
- AWS GovCloud (US)
- US West (N. California)
- US West (Oregon)

Asia Pacific (Tokyo)

Location	How to request a connection
AT Tokyo Chuo Data Center, Tokyo	Requests for cross connects can be submitted by contacting Junko Ikenishi at ikenishi.junko@attokyo.co.jp.
Chief Telecom LY, Taipei	Requests for cross connects can be submitted by contacting Chief Telecom at vicky_chan@chief.com.tw.
Equinix OS1, Osaka	Requests for cross connects can be submitted by contacting Equinix at awsdealreg@equinix.com.

Location	How to request a connection
Equinix TY2, Tokyo	Requests for cross connects can be submitted by contacting Equinix at awsdealreg@equinix.com.

Asia Pacific (Seoul)

Location	How to request a connection
KINX Gasan Data Center, Seoul	Requests for cross connects can be submitted by contacting KINX at sales@kinx.net.
LG U+ Pyeong-Chon Mega Center, Seoul	Requests for cross connects can be made by submitting the LOA document to kidcadmin@lguplus.co.kr and center8@kidc.net.

Asia Pacific (Singapore)

Location	How to request a connection
Equinix SG2, Singapore	Requests for cross connects can be submitted by contacting Equinix at awsdealreg@equinix.com.
Global Switch, Singapore	Requests for cross connects can be submitted by contacting Global Switch at salessingapore@globalswitch.com.
GPX Mumbai	Requests for cross connects can be submitted by contacting GPX at nkankane@gpxglobal.net.
iAdvantage MEGA-i, Hong Kong	Requests for cross connects can be submitted by contacting iAdvantage at cs@iadvantage.net or by placing an order at iAdvantage Cabling Order e-Form.
Menara AIMS, Kuala Lumpur	Existing AIMS customers can request a X-Connect order via the Customer Service portal by filling out the Engineering Work Order Request Form and contacting service.delivery@aims.com.my if there are any problems submitting the request.

Asia Pacific (Sydney)

Location	How to request a connection
Equinix SY3, Sydney	Requests for cross connects can be submitted by contacting Equinix at awsdealreg@equinix.com.
Global Switch SY6, Sydney	Requests for cross connects can be submitted by contacting Global Switch at salessydney@globalswitch.com.
NEXTDC C1, Canberra	Requests for cross connects can be submitted by contacting NEXTDC at nxtops@nextdc.com.

Location	How to request a connection
NEXTDC M1, Melbourne	Requests for cross connects can be submitted by contacting NEXTDC at nxtops@nextdc.com.
NEXTDC P1, Perth	Requests for cross connects can be submitted by contacting NEXTDC at nxtops@nextdc.com.

Asia Pacific (Mumbai)

Location	How to request a connection
GPX Mumbai	Requests for cross connects can be submitted by contacting GPX at nkankane@gpxglobal.net.
NetMagic DC2, Bangalore	Requests for cross connects can be submitted by contacting NetMagic Sales and Marketing toll-free at 18001033130 or at marketing@netmagicsolutions.com.
Sify Rabale, Mumbai	Requests for cross connects can be submitted by contacting Sify at aws.directconnect@sifycorp.com.
STT GDC Pvt. Ltd. VSB, Chennai	Requests for cross connects can be submitted by contacting STT at enquiry.AWSDX@sttelemediagdc.in

Canada (Central)

Location	How to request a connection
Allied 250 Front St W, Toronto	Requests for cross connects can be submitted by contacting driches@alliedreit.com.
Cologix MTL3, Montreal	Requests for cross connects can be submitted by contacting Cologix at aws@cologix.com.
Cologix VAN2, Vancouver	Requests for cross connects can be submitted by contacting Cologix at aws@cologix.com.
eStruxture, Montreal	Requests for cross connects can be submitted by contacting eStruxture at directconnect@estruxture.com.

China (Beijing)

Location	How to request a connection
Sinnet Jiuxianqiao IDC	Requests for cross connects can be submitted by contacting Sinnet at dx-order@sinnet.com.cn.

EU (Frankfurt)

Location	How to request a connection
CE Colo, Prague	Requests for cross connects can be submitted by contacting CE Colo at info@cecolo.com.
Equinix AM3, Amsterdam	Requests for cross connects can be submitted by contacting Equinix at awsdealreg@equinix.com.
Equinix FR5, Frankfurt	Requests for cross connects can be submitted by contacting Equinix at awsdealreg@equinix.com.
Equinix HE6, Helsinki	Requests for cross connects can be submitted by contacting Equinix at awsdealreg@equinix.com.
Equinix ITConic MD2, Madrid	Requests for cross connects can be submitted by contacting Equinix at awsdealreg@equinix.com.
Equinix MU1, Munich	Requests for cross connects can be submitted by contacting Equinix at awsdealreg@equinix.com.
Equinix WA1, Warsaw	Requests for cross connects can be submitted by contacting Equinix at awsdealreg@equinix.com.
IPB, Berlin	Requests for cross connects can be submitted by contacting IPB at kontakt@ipb.de.
Interxion FRA6, Frankfurt	Requests for cross connects can be submitted by contacting Interxion at customer.services@interxion.com.
Interxion MAD2, Madrid	Requests for cross connects can be submitted by contacting Interxion at customer.services@interxion.com.
Interxion MRS1, Marseille	Requests for cross connects can be submitted by contacting Interxion at customer.services@interxion.com.
Interxion STO1, Stockholm	Requests for cross connects can be submitted by contacting Interxion at customer.services@interxion.com.
Interxion VIE2, Vienna	Requests for cross connects can be submitted by contacting Interxion at customer.services@interxion.com.
Interxion ZUR1, Zurich	Requests for cross connects can be submitted by contacting Interxion at customer.services@interxion.com.
Telehouse Voltaire, Paris	Requests for cross connects can be submitted by creating a request at the Customer Portal. Request type: DFM/SFM Layout/Connectivity/MMR Circuit Commissioning

EU (Ireland)

Location	How to request a connection
Digital Realty (UK), Docklands	Requests for cross connects can be submitted by contacting Digital Realty (UK) at amazon.orders@digitalrealty.com.

Location	How to request a connection
Eircom Clonshaugh	Requests for cross connects can be submitted by contacting Eircom at awsorders@eircom.ie.
Equinix LD5, London (Slough)	Requests for cross connects can be submitted by contacting Equinix at awsdealreg@equinix.com.
Interxion DUB2, Dublin	Requests for cross connects can be submitted by contacting Interxion at customer.services@interxion.com.
Interxion MRS1, Marseille	Requests for cross connects can be submitted by contacting Interxion at customer.services@interxion.com.
Teraco CT1, Cape Town	Requests for cross connects can be submitted by contacting Teraco at support@teraco.co.za for existing Teraco customers and connect@teraco.co.za for new customers.
Teraco JB1, Johannesburg	Requests for cross connects can be submitted by contacting Teraco at support@teraco.co.za for existing Teraco customers and connect@teraco.co.za for new customers.

EU (London)

Location	How to request a connection
Digital Realty (UK), Docklands	Requests for cross connects can be submitted by contacting Digital Realty (UK) at amazon.orders@digitalrealty.com.
Equinix LD5, London (Slough)	Requests for cross connects can be submitted by contacting Equinix at awsdealreg@equinix.com.
Equinix MA3, Manchester	Requests for cross connects can be submitted by contacting Equinix at awsdealreg@equinix.com.
Telehouse West, London	Requests for cross-connects can be submitted by contacting Telehouse UK at sales.support@uk.telehouse.net.

EU (Paris)

Location	How to request a connection
Equinix PA3, Paris	Requests for cross connects can be submitted by contacting Equinix at awsdealreg@equinix.com.
Telehouse Voltaire, Paris	Requests for cross connects can be submitted by creating a request at the Customer Portal. Request type: DFM/SFM Layout/Connectivity/MMR Circuit Commissioning

South America (São Paulo)

Location	How to request a connection
Equinix RJ2, Rio de Janeiro	Requests for cross connects can be submitted by contacting Equinix at awsdealreg@equinix.com.
Equinix SP4, São Paulo	Requests for cross connects can be submitted by contacting Equinix at awsdealreg@equinix.com.
Tivit	Requests for cross connects can be submitted by contacting Tivit at aws@tivit.com.br.

US East (N. Virginia)

Location	How to request a connection
165 Halsey Street, Newark	Refer to the resources on http://www.165halsey.com/colocation-services/connectivity/ or contact operations@165halsey.com.
CoreSite NY1, New York	Requests for cross connects can be submitted by placing an order at the CoreSite Customer Portal. After you complete the form, review the order for accuracy, and then approve it using the MyCoreSite website.
CoreSite VA1, Reston	Requests for cross connects can be submitted by placing an order at the CoreSite Customer Portal. After you complete the form, review the order for accuracy, and then approve it using the MyCoreSite website.
Digital Realty ATL1, Atlanta	Requests for cross connects can be submitted by contacting Digital Realty at amazon.orders@digitalrealty.com.
Equinix DC2/DC11, Ashburn	Requests for cross connects can be submitted by contacting Equinix at awsdealreg@equinix.com.
Equinix DA2, Dallas	Requests for cross connects can be submitted by contacting Equinix at awsdealreg@equinix.com.
Equinix MI1, Miami	Requests for cross connects can be submitted by contacting Equinix at awsdealreg@equinix.com.
Lightower, Philadelphia	Requests for cross connects can be submitted by contacting Lightower at awsorders@lightower.com.
Markley, One Summer Street, Boston	Requests for cross connects can be submitted on the customer portal: https://portal.markleygroup.com. For new queries, contact sales@markleygroup.com.

US East (Ohio)

Location	How to request a connection

Location	How to request a connection
Cologix COL2, Columbus	Requests for cross connects can be submitted by contacting Cologix at aws@cologix.com.
Cologix MIN3, Minneapolis	Requests for cross connects can be submitted by contacting Cologix at aws@cologix.com.
CyrusOne West III, Houston	Requests for cross connects and requests for information can be submitted on the customer portal: https://cyrusone.com/about-enterprise-data-center-provider/customer-support/.
Equinix CH2, Chicago	Requests for cross connects can be submitted by contacting Equinix at awsdealreg@equinix.com.
QTS Chicago	Requests for cross connects can be submitted by contacting QTS at AConnect@qtsdatacenters.com.

AWS GovCloud (US)

Location	How to request a connection
Equinix SV5, San Jose	Requests for cross connects can be submitted by contacting Equinix at awsdealreg@equinix.com.

US West (N. California)

Location	How to request a connection
CoreSite LA1, Los Angeles	Requests for cross connects can be submitted by placing an order at the CoreSite Customer Portal. After you complete the form, review the order for accuracy, and then approve it using the MyCoreSite website.
CoreSite SV4, Santa Clara	Requests for cross connects can be submitted by placing an order at the CoreSite Customer Portal. After you complete the form, review the order for accuracy, and then approve it using the MyCoreSite website.
Equinix LA3, El Segundo	Requests for cross connects can be submitted by contacting Equinix at awsdealreg@equinix.com.
Equinix SV5, San Jose	Requests for cross connects can be submitted by contacting Equinix at awsdealreg@equinix.com.
PhoenixNAP, Phoenix	Requests for cross connects can be submitted by contacting phoenixNAP Provisioning at provisioning@phoenixnap.com.

US West (Oregon)

Location	How to request a connection
CoreSite DE1, Denver	Requests for cross connects can be submitted by placing an order at the CoreSite Customer Portal. After you complete the form, review the order for accuracy, and then approve it using the MyCoreSite website.
EdgeConneX, Portland	Requests for cross connects can be submitted by placing an order on the EdgeOS Customer Portal. After you have submitted the form, EdgeConneX will provide a service order form for approval. You can send questions to cloudaccess@edgeconnex.com.
Equinix SE2, Seattle	Requests for cross connects can be submitted by contacting Equinix at support@equinix.com.
Pittock Block, Portland	Requests for cross connects can be submitted by email at crossconnect@pittock.com, or by phone at +1 503 226 6777.
Switch SUPERNAP 8, Las Vegas	Requests for cross connects can be submitted by contacting Switch SUPERNAP at orders@supernap.com.
TierPoint Seattle	Requests for cross connects can be submitted by contacting TierPoint at sales@tierpoint.com.

Virtual Interfaces

You must create a virtual interface to begin using your AWS Direct Connect connection. You can create a private virtual interface to connect to your VPC, or you can create a public virtual interface to connect to AWS services that aren't in a VPC, such as Amazon S3 and Amazon Glacier. You can configure multiple virtual interfaces on a single AWS Direct Connect connection. For private virtual interfaces, you need one private virtual interface for each VPC to connect to from the AWS Direct Connect connection, or you can use a Direct Connect gateway. For more information, see Direct Connect Gateways.

To connect to other AWS services using IPv6 addresses, check the service documentation to verify that IPv6 addressing is supported.

We advertise appropriate Amazon prefixes to you so you can reach either your VPCs or other AWS services. You can access all AWS prefixes through this connection; for example, Amazon EC2, Amazon S3, and Amazon.com. You do not have access to non-Amazon prefixes. For a current list of prefixes advertised by AWS, see AWS IP Address Ranges in the *Amazon Web Services General Reference*.

Note
We recommend that you use a firewall filter (based on the source/destination address of packets) to control traffic to and from some prefixes. If you're using a prefix filter (route map), ensure that it accepts prefixes with an exact match or longer. Prefixes advertised from AWS Direct Connect may be aggregated and may differ from the prefixes defined in your prefix filter.

To use your AWS Direct Connect connection with another AWS account, you can create a hosted virtual interface for that account. The owner of the other account must accept the hosted virtual interface to begin using it. A hosted virtual interface works the same as a standard virtual interface and can connect to public resources or a VPC.

A sub-1G connection only supports one virtual interface.

Topics

- Prerequisites for Virtual Interfaces
- Creating a Virtual Interface
- Viewing Virtual Interface Details
- Deleting a Virtual Interface
- Creating a Hosted Virtual Interface
- Accepting a Hosted Virtual Interface
- Adding or Removing a BGP Peer
- Associating a Virtual Interface with a Connection or LAG

Prerequisites for Virtual Interfaces

To create a virtual interface, you need the following information:

- **Connection**: The AWS Direct Connect connection or link aggregation group (LAG) for which you are creating the virtual interface.
- **Virtual interface name**: A name for the virtual interface.
- **Virtual interface owner**: If you're creating the virtual interface for another account, you need the AWS account ID of the other account.
- (Private virtual interface only) **Connection to**: For connecting to a VPC in the same region, you need the virtual private gateway for your VPC. The ASN for the Amazon side of the BGP session is inherited from the virtual private gateway. When you create a virtual private gateway, you can specify your own private ASN. Otherwise, Amazon provides a default ASN. For more information, see Create a Virtual Private Gateway in the *Amazon VPC User Guide*. For connecting to a VPC through a Direct Connect gateway, you need the Direct Connect gateway. For more information, see Direct Connect Gateways.

- **VLAN**: A unique virtual local area network (VLAN) tag that's not already in use on your connection. The value must be between 1 and 4094 and must comply with the Ethernet 802.1Q standard. This tag is required for any traffic traversing the AWS Direct Connect connection.
- **Address family**: Whether the BGP peering session will be over IPv4 or IPv6.
- **Peer IP addresses**: A virtual interface can support a BGP peering session for IPv4, IPv6, or one of each (dual-stack). You cannot create multiple BGP sessions for the same IP addressing family on the same virtual interface. The IP address ranges are assigned to each end of the virtual interface for the BGP peering session.
    - IPv4:
        - (Public virtual interface only) You must specify unique public IPv4 addresses (/30) that you own.
        - (Private virtual interface only) Amazon can generate private IPv4 addresses for you. If you specify your own, ensure that you specify private CIDRs for your router interface and the AWS Direct Connect interface only (for example, do not specify other IP addresses from your local network).
    - IPv6: Amazon automatically allocates you a /125 IPv6 CIDR. You cannot specify your own peer IPv6 addresses.
- **BGP information**:
    - A public or private Border Gateway Protocol (BGP) Autonomous System Number (ASN) for your side of the BGP session. If you are using a public ASN, you must own it. If you are using a private ASN, it must be in the 64512 to 65535 range. Autonomous System (AS) prepending does not work if you use a private ASN for a public virtual interface.
    - An MD5 BGP authentication key. You can provide your own, or you can let Amazon generate one for you.
- (Public virtual interface only) **Prefixes you want to advertise**: Public IPv4 routes or IPv6 routes to advertise over BGP. You must advertise at least one prefix using BGP, up to a maximum of 1,000 prefixes.
    - IPv4: The IPv4 CIDR must not overlap with another public IPv4 CIDR announced via AWS Direct Connect. If you do not own public IPv4 addresses, your network provider might be able to provide you with a public IPv4 CIDR. If not, contact AWS Support to request a /31 public IPv4 CIDR (and provide a use case in your request).
    - IPv6: Specify a prefix length of /64 or shorter.

Creating a Virtual Interface

You can create a public virtual interface to connect to public resources (non-VPC services), or a private virtual interface to connect to your VPC.

Before you begin, ensure that you have read the information in Prerequisites for Virtual Interfaces.

Creating a Public Virtual Interface

To provision a public virtual interface

1. Open the AWS Direct Connect console at https://console.aws.amazon.com/directconnect/.

2. In the navigation pane, choose **Connections**, select the connection to use, and then choose **Actions**, **Create Virtual Interface**.

3. In the **Create a Virtual Interface** pane, choose **Public**.

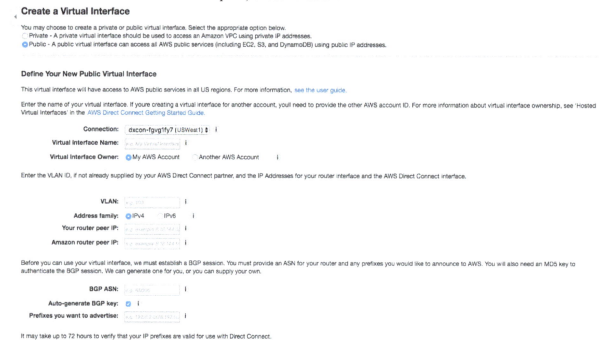

4. In the **Define Your New Public Virtual Interface** dialog box, do the following and choose **Continue**:

   1. For **Connection**, select an existing physical connection on which to create the virtual interface.

   2. For **Virtual Interface Name**, enter a name for the virtual interface.

   3. For **Virtual Interface Owner**, select the **My AWS Account** option if the virtual interface is for your AWS account.

   4. For **VLAN**, enter the ID number for your virtual local area network (VLAN).

   5. If you're configuring an IPv4 BGP peer, choose **IPv4**, and do the following:
      - For **Your router peer IP**, enter the IPv4 CIDR destination address to which Amazon should send traffic.
      - For **Amazon router peer IP**, enter the IPv4 CIDR address to use to send traffic to Amazon.

   6. If you're configuring an IPv6 BGP peer, choose **IPv6**. The peer IPv6 addresses are automatically assigned from Amazon's pool of IPv6 addresses. You cannot specify custom IPv6 addresses.

7. For **BGP ASN**, enter the Border Gateway Protocol (BGP) Autonomous System Number (ASN) of your gateway.

8. To have AWS generate a BGP key, select the **Auto-generate BGP key** check box.

   To provide your own BGP key, clear the **Auto-generate BGP key** check box. For **BGP Authentication Key**, enter your BGP MD5 key.

9. For **Prefixes you want to advertise**, enter the IPv4 CIDR destination addresses (separated by commas) to which traffic should be routed over the virtual interface.

5. Download the router configuration for your device. For more information, see Downloading the Router Configuration File.

To create a public virtual interface using the command line or API

- create-public-virtual-interface (AWS CLI)
- CreatePublicVirtualInterface (AWS Direct Connect API)

Creating a Private Virtual Interface

You can provision a private virtual interface to a virtual private gateway in the same region as your AWS Direct Connect connection. For more information about provisioning a private virtual interface to a direct connect gateway, see Direct Connect Gateways.

To provision a private virtual interface to a VPC

1. Open the AWS Direct Connect console at https://console.aws.amazon.com/directconnect/.

2. In the navigation pane, choose **Connections**, select the connection to use, and choose **Actions**, **Create Virtual Interface**.

3. In the **Create a Virtual Interface** pane, select **Private**.

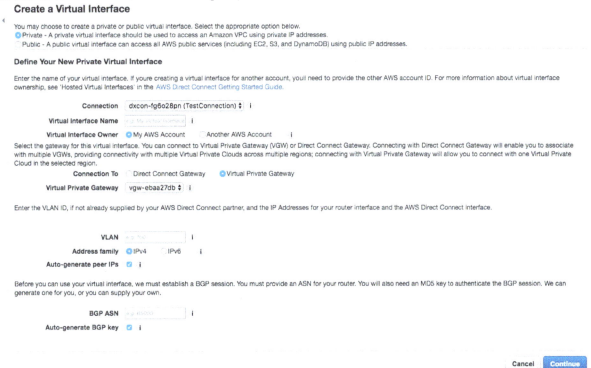

4. Under **Define Your New Private Virtual Interface**, do the following and choose **Continue**:

1. For **Virtual Interface Name**, enter a name for the virtual interface.

2. For **Virtual Interface Owner**, select the **My AWS Account** option if the virtual interface is for your AWS account.

3. For **Connection To**, choose **Virtual Private Gateway** and select the virtual private gateway to which to connect.

4. For **VLAN**, enter the ID number for your virtual local area network (VLAN).

5. If you're configuring an IPv4 BGP peer, choose **IPv4**, and do the following:

   - To have AWS generate your router IP address and Amazon IP address, select **Auto-generate peer IPs**.
   - To specify these IP addresses yourself, clear the **Auto-generate peer IPs** check box. For **Your router peer IP**, enter the destination IPv4 CIDR address to which Amazon should send traffic. For **Amazon router peer IP**, enter the IPv4 CIDR address to use to send traffic to AWS.

6. If you're configuring an IPv6 BGP peer, choose **IPv6**. The peer IPv6 addresses are automatically assigned from Amazon's pool of IPv6 addresses. You cannot specify custom IPv6 addresses.

7. For **BGP ASN**, enter the Border Gateway Protocol (BGP) Autonomous System Number (ASN) of your gateway.

8. To have AWS generate a BGP key, select the **Auto-generate BGP key** check box.

   To provide your own BGP key, clear the **Auto-generate BGP key** check box. For **BGP Authentication Key**, enter your BGP MD5 key.

Note

If you use the VPC wizard to create a VPC, route propagation is automatically enabled for you. With route propagation, routes are automatically populated to the route tables in your VPC. If you choose, you can disable route propagation. For more information, see Enable Route Propagation in Your Route Table in the *Amazon VPC User Guide*.

After you've created the virtual interface, you can download the router configuration for your device. For more information, see Downloading the Router Configuration File.

To create a private virtual interface using the command line or API

- create-private-virtual-interface (AWS CLI)
- CreatePrivateVirtualInterface (AWS Direct Connect API)

Downloading the Router Configuration File

After you've created the virtual interface, you can download the router configuration file for your router.

To download a router configuration

1. Open the AWS Direct Connect console at https://console.aws.amazon.com/directconnect/.

2. In the **Virtual Interfaces** pane, select the virtual interface and then choose **Actions, Download Router Configuration**.

3. In the **Download Router Configuration** dialog box, do the following:

   1. For **Vendor**, select the manufacturer of your router.

   2. For **Platform**, select the model of your router.

   3. For **Software**, select the software version for your router.

4. Choose **Download**, and then use the appropriate configuration for your router to ensure that you can connect to AWS Direct Connect.

Example Router Configuration Files

The following are example extracts of router configuration files.

Cisco IOS

```
1  interface GigabitEthernet0/1
2  no ip address
3
4  interface GigabitEthernet0/1.VLAN_NUMBER
5  description "Direct Connect to your Amazon VPC or AWS Cloud"
6  encapsulation dot1Q VLAN_NUMBER
7  ip address YOUR_PEER_IP
8
9  router bgp CUSTOMER_BGP_ASN
10 neighbor AWS_PEER_IP remote-as AWS_ASN
11 neighbor AWS_PEER_IP password MD5_key
12 network 0.0.0.0
13 exit
14
15 ! Optionally configure Bidirectional Forwarding Detection (BFD).
16
17 interface GigabitEthernet0/1.VLAN_NUMBER
18 bfd interval 300 min_rx 300 multiplier 3
19 router bgp CUSTOMER_BGP_ASN
20 neighbor AWS_PEER_IP fall-over bfd
21
22 ! NAT Configuration for Public Virtual Interfaces (Optional)
23
24 ip access-list standard NAT-ACL
25  permit any
26 exit
27
28 ip nat inside source list NAT-ACL interface GigabitEthernet0/1.VLAN_NUMBER overload
29
30 interface GigabitEthernet0/1.VLAN_NUMBER
31  ip nat outside
32 exit
33
34 interface interface-towards-customer-local-network
35  ip nat inside
36 exit
```

**Cisco NX-OS **

```
1  feature interface-vlan
2  vlan VLAN_NUMBER
3  name "Direct Connect to your Amazon VPC or AWS Cloud"
4
5  interface VlanVLAN_NUMBER
6   ip address YOUR_PEER_IP/30
7   no shutdown
8
9  interface Ethernet0/1
10  switchport
11  switchport mode trunk
```

```
12    switchport trunk allowed vlan VLAN_NUMBER
13    no shutdown
14
15 router bgp CUSTOMER_BGP_ASN
16    address-family ipv4 unicast
17       network 0.0.0.0
18    neighbor AWS_PEER_IP remote-as AWS_ASN
19       password 0 MD5_key
20       address-family ipv4 unicast
21
22 ! Optionally configure Bidirectional Forwarding Detection (BFD).
23
24 feature bfd
25 interface VlanVLAN_NUMBER
26 bfd interval 300 min_rx 300 multiplier 3
27 router bgp CUSTOMER_BGP_ASN
28 neighbor AWS_PEER_IP remote-as AWS_ASN
29 bfd
30
31 ! NAT Configuration for Public Virtual Interfaces (Optional)
32
33 ip access-list standard NAT-ACL
34  permit any any
35 exit
36
37 ip nat inside source list NAT-ACL VlanVLAN_NUMBER overload
38
39 interface VlanVLAN_NUMBER
40  ip nat outside
41 exit
42
43 interface interface-towards-customer-local-network
44  ip nat inside
45 exit
```

Juniper JunOS

```
 1 configure exclusive
 2 edit interfaces ge-0/0/1
 3 set description "Direct Connect to your Amazon VPC or AWS Cloud"
 4 set flexible-vlan-tagging
 5 set mtu 1522
 6 edit unit 0
 7 set vlan-id VLAN_NUMBER
 8 set family inet mtu 1500
 9 set family inet address YOUR_PEER_IP
10 top
11
12 edit policy-options policy-statement EXPORT-DEFAULT
13 edit term DEFAULT
14 set from route-filter 0.0.0.0/0 exact
15 set then accept
16 up
17 edit term REJECT
18 set then reject
```

```
19 top
20
21 set routing-options autonomous-system CUSTOMER_BGP_ASN
22
23 edit protocols bgp group EBGP
24 set type external
25 set peer-as AWS_ASN
26
27 edit neighbor AWS_PEER_IP
28 set local-address YOUR_PEER_IP
29 set export EXPORT-DEFAULT
30 set authentication-key "MD5_key"
31 top
32 commit check
33 commit and-quit
34
35 # Optionally configure Bidirectional Forwarding Detection (BFD).
36
37 set protocols bgp group EBGP neighbor AWS_PEER_IP bfd-liveness-detection minimum-interval 300
38 set protocols bgp group EBGP neighbor AWS_PEER_IP bfd-liveness-detection multiplier 3
39
40 # NAT Configuration for Public Virtual Interfaces (Optional)
41
42 set security policies from-zone trust to-zone untrust policy PolicyName match source-address any
43 set security policies from-zone trust to-zone untrust policy PolicyName match destination-
      address any
44 set security policies from-zone trust to-zone untrust policy PolicyName match application any
45 set security policies from-zone trust to-zone untrust policy PolicyName then permit
46
47 set security nat source rule-set SNAT-RS from zone trust
48 set security nat source rule-set SNAT-RS to zone untrust
49 set security nat source rule-set SNAT-RS rule SNAT-Rule match source-address 0.0.0.0/0
50 set security nat source rule-set SNAT-RS rule SNAT-Rule then source-nat interface
51
52 commit check
53 commit and-quit
```

Viewing Virtual Interface Details

You can view the current status of your virtual interface; the connection state, name, and location; VLAN and BGP details; and peer IP addresses.

To view details about a virtual interface

1. Open the AWS Direct Connect console at https://console.aws.amazon.com/directconnect/.

2. If necessary, change the region in the navigation bar. For more information, see AWS Regions and Endpoints.

3. In the navigation pane, choose **Virtual Interfaces**.

4. In the **Virtual Interfaces** pane, select a virtual interface to view its details.

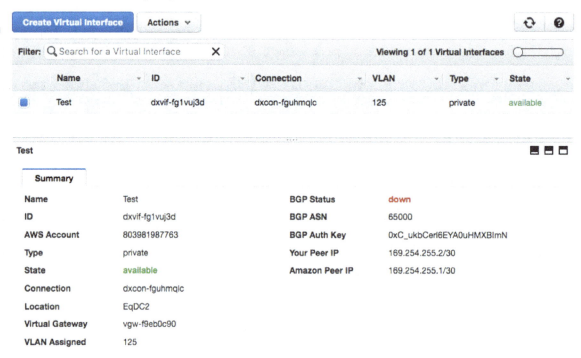

To describe virtual interfaces using the command line or API

- describe-virtual-interfaces (AWS CLI)
- DescribeVirtualInterfaces (AWS Direct Connect API)

Deleting a Virtual Interface

Before you can delete a connection, you must delete its virtual interface. The number of virtual interfaces configured on a connection is listed in the **# VIs** column in the **Connection** pane. Deleting a virtual interface stops AWS Direct Connect data transfer charges associated with the virtual interface.

To delete a virtual interface

1. Open the AWS Direct Connect console at https://console.aws.amazon.com/directconnect/.

2. If necessary, change the region in the navigation bar. For more information, see AWS Regions and Endpoints.

3. In the navigation pane, choose **Virtual Interfaces**.

4. In the **Virtual Interfaces** pane, select a virtual interface, and then choose **Actions, Delete Virtual Interface**.

5. In the **Delete Virtual Interface** dialog box, choose **Delete**.

To delete a virtual interface using the command line or API

- delete-virtual-interface (AWS CLI)
- DeleteVirtualInterface (AWS Direct Connect API)

Creating a Hosted Virtual Interface

You can create a public or private hosted virtual interface. Before you begin, ensure that you have read the information in Prerequisites for Virtual Interfaces.

To create a hosted private virtual interface

1. Open the AWS Direct Connect console at https://console.aws.amazon.com/directconnect/.

2. If necessary, change the region in the navigation bar. For more information, see AWS Regions and Endpoints.

3. In the navigation pane, choose **Connections**.

4. In the **Connections** pane, select the connection to which to add a virtual interface and choose **Actions**, **Create Virtual Interface**.

5. Select the **Private** option.

6. Under **Define Your New Private Virtual Interface**, do the following:

   1. For **Virtual Interface Name**, enter a name for the virtual interface.

   2. For **Virtual Interface Owner**, choose **Another AWS Account**. For **Account ID**, enter the AWS account ID number to associate as the owner of this virtual interface.

   3. For **VLAN**, enter the ID number for your virtual local area network (VLAN).

   4. If you're configuring an IPv4 BGP peer, choose **IPv4**, and do the following:

      - To have AWS generate your router IP address and Amazon IP address, select **Auto-generate peer IPs**.
      - To specify these IP addresses yourself, clear the **Auto-generate peer IPs** check box. For **Your router peer IP**, enter the destination IPv4 CIDR address to which Amazon should send traffic. For **Amazon router peer IP**, enter the IPv4 CIDR address to use to send traffic to AWS.

   5. If you're configuring an IPv6 BGP peer, choose **IPv6**. The peer IPv6 addresses are automatically assigned from Amazon's pool of IPv6 addresses. You cannot specify custom IPv6 addresses.

   6. For **BGP ASN**, enter the Border Gateway Protocol (BGP) Autonomous System Number (ASN) of your gateway.

   7. Select the **Auto-generate BGP key** check box if you would like AWS to generate one for you.

      To provide your own BGP key, clear the **Auto-generate BGP key** check box. For **BGP Authentication Key**, enter your BGP MD5 key.

7. Choose **Continue**. The new interface is added to the list of virtual interfaces on the **Virtual Interfaces** pane.

8. After the hosted virtual interface is accepted by the owner of the other AWS account, you can download the router configuration file.

To create a hosted public virtual interface

1. Open the AWS Direct Connect console at https://console.aws.amazon.com/directconnect/.

2. If necessary, change the region in the navigation bar. For more information, see AWS Regions and Endpoints.

3. In the navigation pane, choose **Connections**.

4. In the **Connections** pane, select the connection to which to add a virtual interface and choose **Actions**, **Create Virtual Interface**.

5. Select the **Public** option.

6. In the **Define Your New Public Virtual Interface** dialog box, do the following:

    1. For **Virtual Interface Name**, enter a name for the virtual interface.

    2. For **Virtual Interface Owner**, choose **Another AWS Account**. For **Account ID**, enter the AWS account ID number to associate as the owner of this virtual interface.

    3. For **VLAN**, enter the ID number for your virtual local area network (VLAN).

    4. If you're configuring an IPv4 BGP peer, choose **IPv4**, and do the following:
        - For **Your router peer IP**, enter the IPv4 CIDR destination address to which Amazon should send traffic.
        - For **Amazon router peer IP**, enter the IPv4 CIDR address to use to send traffic to Amazon.

    5. If you're configuring an IPv6 BGP peer, choose **IPv6**. The peer IPv6 addresses are automatically assigned from Amazon's pool of IPv6 addresses. You cannot specify custom IPv6 addresses.

    6. For **BGP ASN**, enter the Border Gateway Protocol (BGP) Autonomous System Number (ASN) of your gateway.

    7. To have AWS generate a BGP key, select the **Auto-generate BGP key** check box.

       To provide your own BGP key, clear the **Auto-generate BGP key** check box. For **BGP Authentication Key**, enter your BGP MD5 key.

    8. For **Prefixes you want to advertise**, enter the IPv4 CIDR destination addresses (separated by commas) to which traffic should be routed over the virtual interface.

7. Choose **Continue**. The new interface is added to the list of virtual interfaces on the **Virtual Interfaces** pane.

8. After the hosted virtual interface is accepted by the owner of the other AWS account, you can download the router configuration file.

To create a hosted private virtual interface using the command line or API

- allocate-private-virtual-interface (AWS CLI)
- AllocatePrivateVirtualInterface (AWS Direct Connect API)

To create a hosted public virtual interface using the command line or API

- allocate-public-virtual-interface (AWS CLI)
- AllocatePublicVirtualInterface (AWS Direct Connect API)

Accepting a Hosted Virtual Interface

Before you can begin using a hosted virtual interface, you must accept the virtual interface. For a private virtual interface, you must also have an existing virtual private gateway or Direct Connect Gateway.

To accept a hosted virtual interface

1. Open the AWS Direct Connect console at https://console.aws.amazon.com/directconnect/.

2. If necessary, change the region in the navigation bar. For more information, see AWS Regions and Endpoints.

3. In the navigation pane, choose **Virtual Interfaces**.

4. In the **Virtual Interfaces** pane, select the virtual interface to view its details.

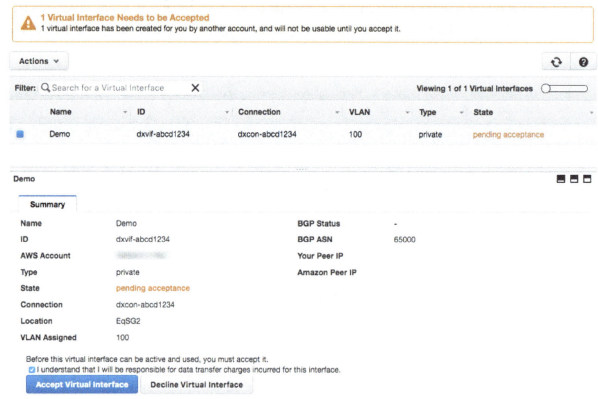

5. Select the **I understand that I will be responsible for data transfer charges incurred for this interface** check box and choose **Accept Virtual Interface**.

6. (Private virtual interface) In the **Accept Virtual Interface** dialog box, select a virtual private gateway or Direct Connect gateway, and choose **Accept**.

7. After you've accepted the hosted virtual interface, the owner of the AWS Direct Connect connection can download the router configuration file. The **Download Router Configuration** option is not available for the account that accepts the hosted virtual interface.

To accept a hosted private virtual interface using the command line or API

- confirm-private-virtual-interface (AWS CLI)
- ConfirmPrivateVirtualInterface (AWS Direct Connect API)

To accept a hosted public virtual interface using the command line or API

- confirm-public-virtual-interface (AWS CLI)

- ConfirmPublicVirtualInterface (AWS Direct Connect API)

Adding or Removing a BGP Peer

A virtual interface can support a single IPv4 BGP peering session and a single IPv6 BGP peering session. You can add an IPv6 BGP peering session to a virtual interface that has an existing IPv4 BGP peering session. Alternately, you can add an IPv4 BGP peering session to a virtual interface that has an existing IPv6 BGP peering session.

You cannot specify your own peer IPv6 addresses for an IPv6 BGP peering session. Amazon automatically allocates you a /125 IPv6 CIDR.

Multiprotocol BGP is not supported. IPv4 and IPv6 operate in dual-stack mode for the virtual interface.

To add a BGP peer

1. Open the AWS Direct Connect console at https://console.aws.amazon.com/directconnect/.

2. In the navigation pane, choose **Virtual Interfaces** and select the virtual interface.

3. Choose **Actions, Add Peering**.

4. (Private virtual interface) To add an IPv4 BGP peer, do the following:

   - To have AWS generate your router IP address and Amazon IP address, select **Auto-generate peer IPs**.
   - To specify these IP addresses yourself, clear the **Auto-generate peer IPs** check box. For **Your router peer IP**, enter the destination IPv4 CIDR address to which Amazon should send traffic. In the **Amazon router peer IP** field, enter the IPv4 CIDR address to use to send traffic to AWS.

5. (Public virtual interface) To add an IPv4 BGP peer, do the following:

   - For **Your router peer IP**, enter the IPv4 CIDR destination address where traffic should be sent.
   - For **Amazon router peer IP**, enter the IPv4 CIDR address to use to send traffic to AWS.

6. (Private or public virtual interface) To add an IPv6 BGP peer, the **Auto-generate peer IPs** is selected by default. The peer IPv6 addresses are automatically assigned from Amazon's pool of IPv6 addresses; you cannot specify custom IPv6 addresses.

7. In the **BGP ASN** field, enter the Border Gateway Protocol (BGP) Autonomous System Number (ASN) of your gateway; for example, a number between 1 and 65534. For a public virtual interface, the ASN

must be private or already whitelisted for the virtual interface.

8. Select the **Auto-generate BGP key** check box to have AWS to generate one for you.

   To provide your own BGP key, clear the **Auto-generate BGP key** check box. For **BGP Authentication Key**, enter your BGP MD5 key.

9. Choose **Continue**.

If your virtual interface has both an IPv4 and IPv6 BGP peering session, you can delete one of the BGP peering sessions (but not both).

To delete a BGP peer

1. Open the AWS Direct Connect console at https://console.aws.amazon.com/directconnect/.

2. In the navigation pane, choose **Virtual Interfaces** and select the virtual interface.

3. Choose **Actions, Delete Peering**.

4. To delete the IPv4 BGP peer, choose **IPv4**. To delete the IPv6 BGP peer, choose **IPv6**.

5. Choose **Delete**.

To create a BGP peer using the command line or API

- create-bgp-peer (AWS CLI)
- CreateBGPPeer (AWS Direct Connect API)

To delete a BGP peer using the command line or API

- delete-bgp-peer (AWS CLI)
- DeleteBGPPeer (AWS Direct Connect API)

Associating a Virtual Interface with a Connection or LAG

You can associate a virtual interface with a link aggregation group (LAG), or another connection.

You cannot associate a virtual interface if the target connection or LAG has an existing associated virtual interface with the following matching attributes:

- A conflicting VLAN number
- (Public virtual interfaces) The same IP address range for the Amazon router, or for the customer router
- (Private virtual interfaces) The same virtual private gateway and the same IP address range for the Amazon router, or for the customer router

You cannot disassociate a virtual interface from a connection or LAG, but you can re-associate it or delete it. For more information, see Deleting a Virtual Interface.

Important
Connectivity to AWS is temporarily interrupted during the association process.

To associate a virtual interface with a connection

1. Open the AWS Direct Connect console at https://console.aws.amazon.com/directconnect/.

2. In the navigation pane, choose **Virtual Interfaces**, and select the virtual interface.

3. Choose **Actions, Associate Connection or LAG**.

4. Choose the required connection, select the confirmation check box, and choose **Continue**.

You can use the same procedure above to associate a virtual interface with a LAG. Alternatively, you can use the **LAGs** screen.

To associate a virtual interface with a LAG

1. Open the AWS Direct Connect console at https://console.aws.amazon.com/directconnect/.

2. In the navigation pane, choose **LAGs**, and select the LAG.

3. Choose **Actions, Associate Virtual Interface**.

4. Choose the required virtual interface, select the confirmation check box, and choose **Continue**.

To associate a virtual interface using the command line or API

- associate-virtual-interface (AWS CLI)
- AssociateVirtualInterface (AWS Direct Connect API)

Link Aggregation Groups

A link aggregation group (LAG) is a logical interface that uses the Link Aggregation Control Protocol (LACP) to aggregate multiple 1 gigabit or 10 gigabit connections at a single AWS Direct Connect endpoint, allowing you to treat them as a single, managed connection.

You can create a LAG from existing connections, or you can provision new connections. After you've created the LAG, you can associate existing connections (whether standalone or part of another LAG) with the LAG.

The following rules apply:

- All connections in the LAG must use the same bandwidth. The following bandwidths are supported: 1 Gbps and 10 Gbps.
- You can have a maximum of 4 connections in a LAG. Each connection in the LAG counts towards your overall connection limit for the region.
- All connections in the LAG must terminate at the same AWS Direct Connect endpoint.

When you create a LAG, you can download the Letter of Authorization and Connecting Facility Assignment (LOA-CFA) for each new physical connection individually from the AWS Direct Connect console. For more information, see Downloading the LOA-CFA.

All LAGs have an attribute that determines the minimum number of connections in the LAG that must be operational for the LAG itself to be operational. By default, new LAGs have this attribute set to 0. You can update your LAG to specify a different value—doing so means that your entire LAG becomes non-operational if the number of operational connections falls below this threshold. This attribute can be used to prevent over-utilization of the remaining connections.

All connections in a LAG operate in Active/Active mode.

Note
When you create a LAG or associate more connections with the LAG, we may not be able to guarantee enough available ports on a given AWS Direct Connect endpoint.

Topics

- Creating a LAG
- Updating a LAG
- Associating a Connection with a LAG
- Disassociating a Connection From a LAG
- Deleting a LAG

Creating a LAG

You can create a LAG by provisioning new connections, or aggregating existing connections.

You cannot create a LAG with new connections if this results in you exceeding the overall connections limit for the region.

To create a LAG with new connections

1. Open the AWS Direct Connect console at https://console.aws.amazon.com/directconnect/.

2. In the navigation pane, choose **LAGs**, **Create LAG**.

3. Choose **Request new Connections**, and provide the following information.

   - **Location**: Select the location for the LAG.
   - **LAG Name**: Specify a name for the LAG.
   - **Connection Bandwidth**: Select the port speed for the connections.
   - **Number of new Connections**: Specify the number of connections that must be provisioned in the LAG.

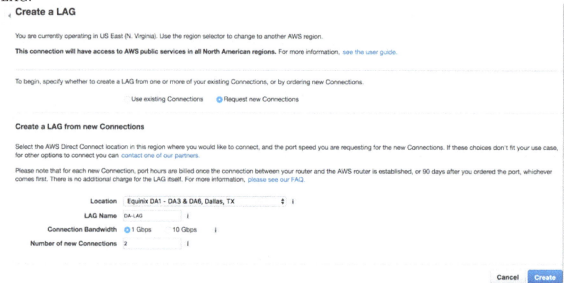

4. Choose **Create**.

To create a LAG from existing connections, the connections must be on the same AWS device (terminate at the same AWS Direct Connect endpoint), and they must use the same bandwidth. You cannot migrate a connection from an existing LAG if removing the connection causes the original LAG to fall below its setting for minimum number of operational connections.

Important
For existing connections, connectivity to AWS is interrupted during the creation of the LAG.

To create a LAG from existing connections

1. Open the AWS Direct Connect console at https://console.aws.amazon.com/directconnect/.

2. In the navigation pane, choose **LAGs**, **Create LAG**.

3. Choose **Use existing Connections**, and select the required connections.

4. For **LAG Name**, specify a name for the LAG. For **Set Minimum Links**, specify the minimum number of connections that must be operational for the LAG itself to be operational. If you do not specify a value,

we assign a default value of 0.

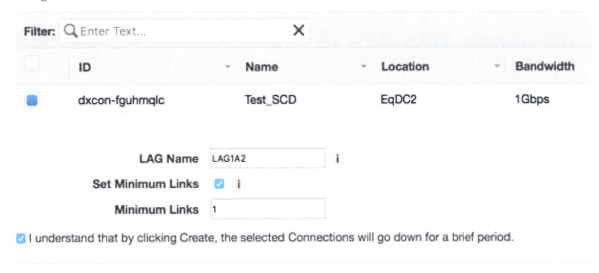

5. Select the confirmation check box and choose **Create**.

After you've created a LAG, you can view its details in the AWS Direct Connect console.

To view information about your LAG

1. Open the AWS Direct Connect console at https://console.aws.amazon.com/directconnect/.

2. In the navigation pane, choose **LAGs**, and select the LAG.

3. You can view information about the LAG, including its ID, the AWS Direct Connect endpoint on which the connections terminate (**AWS Device**), and the number of connections in the LAG (**Port Count**).

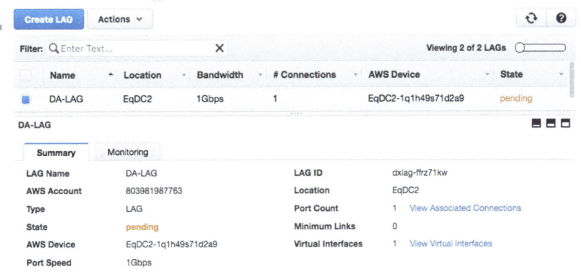

After you've created a LAG, you can associate or disassociate connections from it. For more information, see Associating a Connection with a LAG and Disassociating a Connection From a LAG.

To create a LAG using the command line or API

- create-lag (AWS CLI)
- CreateLag (AWS Direct Connect API)

To describe your LAGs using the command line or API

- describe-lags (AWS CLI)

- DescribeLags (AWS Direct Connect API)

To download the LOA-CFA using the command line or API

- describe-loa (AWS CLI)
- DescribeLoa (AWS Direct Connect API)

Updating a LAG

You can update a LAG to change its name, or to change the value for the minimum number of operational connections.

Note
If you adjust the threshold value for the minimum number if operational connections, ensure that the new value does not cause the LAG to fall below the threshold and become non-operational.

To update a LAG

1. Open the AWS Direct Connect console at https://console.aws.amazon.com/directconnect/.

2. In the navigation pane, choose **LAGs**, and select the LAG.

3. Choose **Actions, Update LAG**.

4. For **LAG Name**, specify a new name for the LAG. For **Minimum Links**, adjust the value for the minimum number of operational connections.

5. Choose **Continue**.

To update a LAG using the command line or API

- update-lag (AWS CLI)
- UpdateLag (AWS Direct Connect API)

Associating a Connection with a LAG

You can associate an existing connection with a LAG. The connection can be standalone, or it can be part of another LAG. The connection must be on the same AWS device and must use the same bandwidth as the LAG. If the connection is already associated with another LAG, you cannot re-associate it if removing the connection causes the original LAG to fall below its threshold for minimum number of operational connections.

Associating a connection to a LAG automatically re-associates its virtual interfaces to the LAG.

Important
Connectivity to AWS over the connection is interrupted during association.

To associate a connection with a LAG

1. Open the AWS Direct Connect console at https://console.aws.amazon.com/directconnect/.

2. In the navigation pane, choose **LAGs**, and select the LAG.

3. Choose **Actions, Associate Connection**.

4. Select the connection from the list of available connections.

5. Select the confirmation check box and choose **Continue**.

To associate a connection using the command line or API

- associate-connection-with-lag (AWS CLI)
- AssociateConnectionWithLag (AWS Direct Connect API)

Disassociating a Connection From a LAG

You can disassociate a connection from a LAG to convert it to a standalone connection. You cannot disassociate a connection if this will cause the LAG to fall below its threshold for minimum number of operational connections.

Disassociating a connection from a LAG does not automatically disassociate any virtual interfaces. You must associate the virtual interface with the connection separately. For more information, see Associating a Virtual Interface with a Connection or LAG.

Important
Connectivity to AWS over the connection is interrupted during disassociation.

To disassociate a connection from a LAG

1. Open the AWS Direct Connect console at https://console.aws.amazon.com/directconnect/.

2. In the navigation pane, choose **LAGs**, and select the LAG.

3. Choose **Actions**, **Disassociate Connection**.

4. Select the connection from the list of available connections.

5. Select the confirmation check box, and choose **Continue**.

To disassociate a connection using the command line or API

- disassociate-connection-from-lag (AWS CLI)
- DisassociateConnectionFromLag (AWS Direct Connect API)

Deleting a LAG

If you no longer need a LAG, you can delete it. You cannot delete a LAG if it has virtual interfaces associated with it—you must first delete the virtual interfaces, or associate them with a different LAG or connection. Deleting a LAG does not delete the connections in the LAG; you must delete the connections yourself. For more information, see Deleting a Connection.

To delete a LAG

1. Open the AWS Direct Connect console at https://console.aws.amazon.com/directconnect/.

2. In the navigation pane, choose **LAGs**, and select the LAG.

3. Choose **Actions**, **Delete LAG**.

4. Select the confirmation check box and choose **Continue**.

To delete a LAG using the command line or API

- delete-lag (AWS CLI)
- DeleteLag (AWS Direct Connect API)

Direct Connect Gateways

You can use an *AWS Direct Connect gateway* to connect your AWS Direct Connect connection over a private virtual interface to one or more VPCs in your account that are located in the same or different regions. You associate a Direct Connect gateway with the virtual private gateway for the VPC, and then create a private virtual interface for your AWS Direct Connect connection to the Direct Connect gateway. You can attach multiple private virtual interfaces to your Direct Connect gateway.

A Direct Connect gateway is a globally available resource. You can create the Direct Connect gateway in any public region and access it from all other public regions.

In the following diagram, the Direct Connect gateway enables you to use your AWS Direct Connect connection in the US East (N. Virginia) region to access VPCs in your account in both the US East (N. Virginia) and US West (N. California) regions.

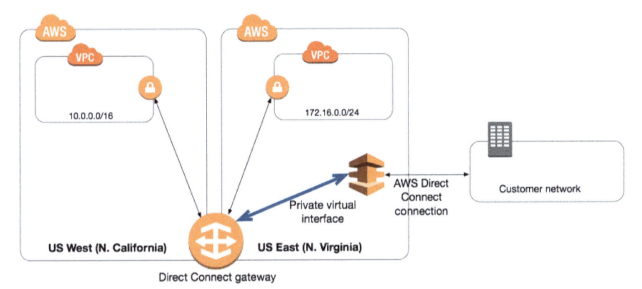

The following rules apply:

- You cannot use a Direct Connect gateway to connect to a VPC in the China regions.
- You cannot use a Direct Connect gateway that's in your account to connect to a VPC that's in a different AWS account. To associate a Direct Connect gateway with a virtual private gateway, it must be in the same account as the virtual private gateway.
- There are limits for creating and using Direct Connect gateways. For more information, see AWS Direct Connect Limits.
- The VPCs to which you connect through a Direct Connect gateway cannot have overlapping CIDR blocks. If you add an IPv4 CIDR block to a VPC that's associated with a Direct Connect gateway, ensure that the CIDR block does not overlap with an existing CIDR block for any other associated VPC. For more information, see Adding IPv4 CIDR Blocks to a VPC in the *Amazon VPC User Guide*.
- You cannot create a public virtual interface to a Direct Connect gateway.
- A Direct Connect gateway supports communication between attached private virtual interfaces and associated virtual private gateways only. The following traffic flows are not supported:
  - Direct communication between the VPCs that are associated with the Direct Connect gateway.
  - Direct communication between the virtual interfaces that are attached to the Direct Connect gateway.
  - Direct communication between a virtual interface attached to a Direct Connect gateway and a VPN connection on a virtual private gateway that's associated with the same Direct Connect gateway.
- You cannot associate a virtual private gateway with more than one Direct Connect gateway and you cannot attach a private virtual interface to more than one Direct Connect gateway.
- A virtual private gateway that you associate with a Direct Connect gateway must be attached to a VPC.

- You cannot tag a Direct Connect gateway.

To connect your AWS Direct Connect connection to a VPC in the same region only, you can create a Direct Connect gateway or you can create a private virtual interface and attach it to the virtual private gateway for the VPC. For more information, see Creating a Private Virtual Interface and VPN CloudHub.

To use your AWS Direct Connect connection with a VPC in another account, you can create a hosted private virtual interface for that account. When the owner of the other account accepts the hosted virtual interface, they can choose to attach it to either a virtual private gateway or a Direct Connect gateway in their account. For more information, see Virtual Interfaces.

Topics

- Creating a Direct Connect Gateway
- Associating and Disassociating Virtual Private Gateways
- Creating a Private Virtual Interface to the Direct Connect Gateway
- Deleting a Direct Connect Gateway

Creating a Direct Connect Gateway

You can create a Direct Connect gateway in any supported public region.

To create a Direct Connect gateway

1. Open the AWS Direct Connect console at https://console.aws.amazon.com/directconnect/.

2. In the navigation pane, choose **Direct Connect Gateways**.

3. Choose **Create Direct Connect Gateway**.

4. Specify the following information, and choose **Create**.

   - **Name**: Enter a name to help you identify the Direct Connect gateway.
   - **Amazon side ASN**: Specify the ASN for the Amazon side of the BGP session. The ASN must be in the 64,512 to 65,534 range or 4,200,000,000 to 4,294,967,294 range.

To create a Direct Connect gateway using the command line or API

- create-direct-connect-gateway (AWS CLI)
- CreateDirectConnectGateway (AWS Direct Connect API)

Associating and Disassociating Virtual Private Gateways

To associate a virtual private gateway with a Direct Connect gateway, you must be in the region in which the virtual private gateway is located. The virtual private gateway must be attached to the VPC to which you want to connect. For more information, see Create a Virtual Private Gateway in the *Amazon VPC User Guide*.

Note
If you are planning to use the virtual private gateway for a Direct Connect gateway and a dynamic VPN connection, set the ASN on the virtual private gateway to the value you require for the VPN connection. Otherwise, the ASN on the virtual private gateway can be set to any permitted value. The Direct Connect gateway advertises all connected VPCs over the ASN assigned to it.

To associate a virtual private gateway

1. Open the AWS Direct Connect console at https://console.aws.amazon.com/directconnect/.

2. Use the region selector to select the region in which your virtual private gateway is located.

3. In the navigation pane, choose **Direct Connect Gateways** and select the Direct Connect gateway.

4. Choose **Actions, Associate Virtual Private Gateway**.

5. Select the virtual private gateways to associate, and choose **Associate**.

You can view all the virtual private gateways in all regions that are associated with the Direct Connect gateway by choosing **Virtual Gateway Associations**. To disassociate a virtual private gateway from a Direct Connect gateway, you must be in the region in which the virtual private gateway is located.

To disassociate a virtual private gateway

1. Open the AWS Direct Connect console at https://console.aws.amazon.com/directconnect/.

2. Use the region selector to switch to the region in which your virtual private gateway is located.

3. In the navigation pane, choose **Direct Connect Gateways** and select the Direct Connect gateway.

4. Choose **Actions, Disassociate Virtual Private Gateway**.

5. Select the virtual private gateways to disassociate, and choose **Disassociate**.

To associate a virtual private gateway using the command line or API

- create-direct-connect-gateway-association (AWS CLI)
- CreateDirectConnectGatewayAssociation (AWS Direct Connect API)

To view the virtual private gateways associated with a Direct Connect gateway using the command line or API

- describe-direct-connect-gateway-associations (AWS CLI)
- DescribeDirectConnectGatewayAssociations (AWS Direct Connect API)

To disassociate a virtual private gateway using the command line or API

- delete-direct-connect-gateway-association (AWS CLI)
- DeleteDirectConnectGatewayAssociation (AWS Direct Connect API)

Creating a Private Virtual Interface to the Direct Connect Gateway

To connect your AWS Direct Connect connection to the remote VPC, you must create a private virtual interface for your connection and specify the Direct Connect gateway to which to connect.

Note
If you're accepting a hosted private virtual interface, you can associate it with a Direct Connect gateway in your account. For more information, see Accepting a Hosted Virtual Interface.

To provision a private virtual interface to a Direct Connect gateway

1. Open the AWS Direct Connect console at https://console.aws.amazon.com/directconnect/.

2. In the navigation pane, choose **Connections**, select the connection to use, and choose **Actions, Create Virtual Interface**.

3. In the **Create a Virtual Interface** pane, select **Private**.

Create a Virtual Interface

You may choose to create a private or public virtual interface. Select the appropriate option below.

○ Private - A private virtual interface should be used to access an Amazon VPC using private IP addresses.
○ Public - A public virtual interface can access all AWS public services (including EC2, S3, and DynamoDB) using public IP addresses.

Define Your New Private Virtual Interface

Enter the name of your virtual interface. If youre creating a virtual interface for another account, youll need to provide the other AWS account ID. For more information about virtual interface ownership, see 'Hosted Virtual Interfaces' in the AWS Direct Connect Getting Started Guide.

Connection	dxcon-fg6o28pn (TestConnection) ⬍ ℹ
Virtual Interface Name	e.g. My Virtual Interface ℹ
Virtual Interface Owner	● My AWS Account ○ Another AWS Account ℹ

Select the gateway for this virtual interface. You can connect to Virtual Private Gateway (VGW) or Direct Connect Gateway. Connecting with Direct Connect Gateway will enable you to associate with multiple VGWs, providing connectivity with multiple Virtual Private Clouds across multiple regions; connecting with Virtual Private Gateway will allow you to connect with one Virtual Private Cloud in the selected region.

Connection To	● Direct Connect Gateway ○ Virtual Private Gateway
Direct Connect Gateway	MyDxGateway ⬍ ℹ
	Create Direct Connect Gateway

Enter the VLAN ID, if not already supplied by your AWS Direct Connect partner, and the IP Addresses for your router interface and the AWS Direct Connect interface.

VLAN	e.g. 100 ℹ
Address family	● IPv4 ○ IPv6 ℹ
Auto-generate peer IPs	☑ ℹ

Before you can use your virtual interface, we must establish a BGP session. You must provide an ASN for your router. You will also need an MD5 key to authenticate the BGP session. We can generate one for you, or you can supply your own.

BGP ASN	e.g. 65000 ℹ
Auto-generate BGP key	☑ ℹ

Cancel **Continue**

4. Under **Define Your New Private Virtual Interface**, do the following and choose **Continue**:

   1. For **Virtual Interface Name**, enter a name for the virtual interface.

   2. For **Virtual Interface Owner**, select the **My AWS Account** option if the virtual interface is for your AWS account.

   3. For **Connection To**, choose **Direct Connect Gateway** and select the Direct Connect gateway.

   4. For **VLAN**, enter the ID number for your virtual local area network (VLAN).

   5. If you're configuring an IPv4 BGP peer, choose **IPv4**, and do the following:

      - To have AWS generate your router IP address and Amazon IP address, select **Auto-generate peer IPs**.
      - To specify these IP addresses yourself, clear the **Auto-generate peer IPs** check box. For **Your router peer IP**, enter the destination IPv4 CIDR address to which Amazon should send traffic. For **Amazon router peer IP**, enter the IPv4 CIDR address to use to send traffic to AWS.

   6. If you're configuring an IPv6 BGP peer, choose **IPv6**. The peer IPv6 addresses are automatically assigned from Amazon's pool of IPv6 addresses. You cannot specify custom IPv6 addresses.

   7. For **BGP ASN**, enter the Border Gateway Protocol (BGP) Autonomous System Number (ASN) of your gateway.

   8. To have AWS generate a BGP key, select the **Auto-generate BGP key** check box .

      To provide your own BGP key, clear the **Auto-generate BGP key** check box. For **BGP Authentication Key**, enter your BGP MD5 key.

After you've created the virtual interface, you can download the router configuration for your device. For more information, see Downloading the Router Configuration File.

To create a private virtual interface using the command line or API

- create-private-virtual-interface (AWS CLI)
- CreatePrivateVirtualInterface (AWS Direct Connect API)

To view the virtual interfaces that are attached to a Direct Connect gateway using the command line or API

- describe-direct-connect-gateway-attachments (AWS CLI)
- DescribeDirectConnectGatewayAttachments (AWS Direct Connect API)

Deleting a Direct Connect Gateway

If you no longer require a Direct Connect gateway, you can delete it. You must first disassociate all associated virtual private gateways and delete the attached private virtual interface.

To delete a Direct Connect gateway

1. Open the AWS Direct Connect console at https://console.aws.amazon.com/directconnect/.

2. In the navigation pane, choose **Direct Connect Gateways** and select the Direct Connect gateway.

3. Choose **Actions, Delete Direct Connect Gateway**.

4. Choose **Delete**.

To delete a Direct Connect gateway using the command line or API

- delete-direct-connect-gateway (AWS CLI)
- DeleteDirectConnectGateway (AWS Direct Connect API)

Using AWS Identity and Access Management with AWS Direct Connect

You can use AWS Identity and Access Management with AWS Direct Connect to specify which AWS Direct Connect actions a user under your AWS account can perform. For example, you could create an IAM policy that gives only certain users in your organization permission to use the `DescribeConnections` action to retrieve data about your AWS Direct Connect connections.

Permissions granted using IAM cover all the AWS resources you use with AWS Direct Connect, so you cannot use IAM to control access to AWS Direct Connect data for specific resources. For example, you cannot give a user access to AWS Direct Connect data for only a specific virtual interface.

Important
Using AWS Direct Connect with IAM doesn't change how you use AWS Direct Connect. There are no changes to AWS Direct Connect actions, and no new AWS Direct Connect actions related to users and access control. For an example of a policy that covers AWS Direct Connect actions, see Example Policy for AWS Direct Connect.

AWS Direct Connect Actions

In an IAM policy, you can specify any or all actions that AWS Direct Connect offers. The action name must include the lowercase prefix `directconnect:`. For example: `directconnect:DescribeConnections`, `directconnect:CreateConnection`, or `directconnect:*` (for all AWS Direct Connect actions). For a list of the actions, see the *AWS Direct Connect API Reference*.

AWS Direct Connect Resources

AWS Direct Connect does not support resource-level permissions; therefore, you cannot control access to specific AWS Direct Connect resources. You must use an asterisk (*) to specify the resource when writing a policy to control access to AWS Direct Connect actions.

AWS Direct Connect Keys

AWS Direct Connect implements the following policy keys:

- `aws:CurrentTime` (for date/time conditions)
- `aws:EpochTime` (the date in epoch or UNIX time, for use with date/time conditions)
- `aws:SecureTransport` (Boolean representing whether the request was sent using SSL)
- `aws:SourceIp` (the requester's IP address, for use with IP address conditions)
- `aws:UserAgent` (information about the requester's client application, for use with string conditions)

If you use `aws:SourceIp`, and the request comes from an Amazon EC2 instance, the instance's public IP address is used to determine if access is allowed.

Note
For services that use only SSL, such as Amazon Relational Database Service and Amazon Route 53, the `aws:SecureTransport` key has no meaning.

Key names are case-insensitive. For example, `aws:CurrentTime` is equivalent to `AWS:currenttime`.

For more information about policy keys, see Condition in *IAM User Guide*.

Example Policy for AWS Direct Connect

This section shows a simple policy for controlling user access to AWS Direct Connect.

Note
In the future, AWS Direct Connect might add new actions that should logically be included in the following policy, based on the policy's stated goals.

Example

The following sample policy allows a group to retrieve any AWS Direct Connect data, but not create or delete any resources.

```
1  {
2    "Statement": [
3      {
4        "Effect": "Allow",
5        "Action": [
6          "directconnect:Describe*"
7        ],
8        "Resource": "*"
9      }
10   ]
11 }
```

For more information about writing IAM policies, see Overview of IAM Policies in the *IAM User Guide*.

Using Tags with AWS Direct Connect

You can optionally assign tags to your AWS Direct Connect resources to categorize or manage them. A tag consists of a key and an optional value, both of which you define.

You can tag the following AWS Direct Connect resources.

Resource	Amazon Resource Name (ARN)
Connections	arn:aws:directconnect:region:account-id:dxcon/connection-id
Virtual interfaces	arn:aws:directconnect:region:account-id:dxvif/virtual-interface-id
Link aggregation group (LAG)	arn:aws:directconnect:region:account-id:dxlag/lag-id

For example, you have two AWS Direct Connect connections in a region, each in different locations. Connection `dxcon-11aa22bb` is a connection serving production traffic, and is associated with virtual interface `dxvif-33 cc44dd`. Connection `dxcon-abcabcab` is a redundant (backup) connection, and is associated with virtual interface `dxvif-12312312`. You might choose to tag your connections and virtual interfaces as follows, to help distinguish them:

[See the AWS documentation website for more details]

Tag Restrictions

The following rules and restrictions apply to tags:

- Maximum number of tags per resource: 50
- Maximum key length: 128 Unicode characters
- Maximum value length: 265 Unicode characters
- Tag keys and values are case sensitive.
- The `aws:` prefix is reserved for AWS use — you can't create or delete tag keys or values with this prefix. Tags with this prefix do not count against your tags per resource limit.
- Allowed characters are letters, spaces, and numbers representable in UTF-8, plus the following special characters: + - = . _ : / @
- Cost allocation tags are not supported; therefore, tags that you apply to AWS Direct Connect resources cannot be used for cost allocation tracking.

Working with Tags

Currently, you can work with tags using the AWS Direct Connect API, the AWS CLI, the AWS Tools for Windows PowerShell, or an AWS SDK only. To apply or remove tags, you must specify the Amazon Resource Name (ARN) for the resource. For more information, see Amazon Resource Names (ARNs) and AWS Service Namespaces in the *Amazon Web Services General Reference*.

To add a tag using the AWS CLI

Use the tag-resource command:

```
1 aws directconnect tag-resource --resource-arn arn:aws:directconnect:region:account-id:resource-
    type/resource-id --tags "key=key,value=value"
```

To describe your tags using the AWS CLI

Use the describe-tags command:

```
1 aws directconnect describe-tags --resource-arns arn:aws:directconnect:region:account-id:resource
    -type/resource-id
```

To delete a tag using the AWS CLI

Use the untag-resource command:

```
1 aws directconnect untag-resource --resource-arn arn:aws:directconnect:region:account-id:resource
    -type/resource-id --tag-keys key
```

Using the AWS CLI

You can use the AWS CLI to create and work with AWS Direct Connect resources.

The following example uses the AWS CLI commands to create an AWS Direct Connect connection, download the Letter of Authorization and Connecting Facility Assignment (LOA-CFA), and provision a private or public virtual interface.

Before you begin, ensure that you have installed and configured the AWS CLI. For more information, see the AWS Command Line Interface User Guide.

Topics

- Step 1: Create a Connection
- Step 2: Download the LOA-CFA
- Step 3: Create a Virtual Interface and get the Router Configuration

Step 1: Create a Connection

The first step is to submit a connection request. Ensure that you know the port speed that you require and the AWS Direct Connect location. For more information, see Connections.

To create a connection request

1. Describe the AWS Direct Connect locations for your current region. In the output that's returned, take note of the location code for the location in which you want to establish the connection.

```
aws directconnect describe-locations
```

```
{
    "locations": [
        {
            "locationName": "NAP do Brasil, Barueri, Sao Paulo",
            "locationCode": "TNDB"
        },
        {
            "locationName": "Tivit - Site Transamerica (Sao Paulo)",
            "locationCode": "TIVIT"
        }
    ]
}
```

2. Create the connection and specify a name, the port speed, and the location code. In the output that's returned, take note of the connection ID. You need the ID to get the LOA-CFA in the next step.

```
aws directconnect create-connection --location TIVIT --bandwidth 1Gbps --connection-name "
    Connection to AWS"
```

```
{
    "ownerAccount": "123456789012",
    "connectionId": "dxcon-fg31dyv6",
    "connectionState": "requested",
    "bandwidth": "1Gbps",
    "location": "TIVIT",
    "connectionName": "Connection to AWS",
    "region": "sa-east-1"
}
```

Step 2: Download the LOA-CFA

After you've requested a connection, you can get the LOA-CFA using the `describe-loa` command. The output is base64-encoded. You must extract the relevant LOA content, decode it, and create a PDF file.

To get the LOA-CFA using Linux or Mac OS X

In this example, the final part of the command decodes the content using the base64 utility, and sends the output to a PDF file.

```
1 aws directconnect describe-loa --connection-id dxcon-fg31dyv6 --output text --query loaContent|
    base64 --decode > myLoaCfa.pdf
```

To get the LOA-CFA using Windows

In this example, the output is extracted to a file called myLoaCfa.base64. The second command uses the `certutil` utility to decode the file and send the output to a PDF file.

```
1 aws directconneawsct describe-loa --connection-id dxcon-fg31dyv6 --output text --query
    loaContent > myLoaCfa.base64
```

```
1 certutil -decode myLoaCfa.base64 myLoaCfa.pdf
```

After you've downloaded the LOA-CFA, send it to your network provider or colocation provider.

Step 3: Create a Virtual Interface and get the Router Configuration

After you have placed an order for an AWS Direct Connect connection, you must create a virtual interface to begin using it. You can create a private virtual interface to connect to your VPC, or you can create a public virtual interface to connect to AWS services that aren't in a VPC. You can create a virtual interface that supports IPv4 or IPv6 traffic.

Before you begin, ensure that you've read the prerequisites in Prerequisites for Virtual Interfaces.

When you create a virtual interface using the AWS CLI, the output includes generic router configuration information. If you want router configuration that's specific to your device, use the AWS Direct Connect console. For more information, see Downloading the Router Configuration File.

To create a private virtual interface

1. Get the ID of the virtual private gateway (vgw-*xxxxxxxx*) that's attached to your VPC. You need the ID to create the virtual interface in the next step.

```
1 aws ec2 describe-vpn-gateways
```

```
1  {
2      "VpnGateways": [
3          {
4              "State": "available",
5              "Tags": [
6                  {
7                      "Value": "DX_VGW",
8                      "Key": "Name"
9                  }
10             ],
11             "Type": "ipsec.1",
12             "VpnGatewayId": "vgw-ebaa27db",
13             "VpcAttachments": [
14                 {
```

```
15                "State": "attached",
16                "VpcId": "vpc-24f33d4d"
17            }
18        ]
19    }
20  ]
21 }
```

2. Create a private virtual interface. You must specify a name, a VLAN ID, and a BGP Autonomous System Number (ASN).

For IPv4 traffic, you need private IPv4 addresses for each end of the BGP peering session. You can specify your own IPv4 addresses, or you can let Amazon generate the addresses for you. In the following example, the IPv4 addresses are generated for you.

```
1 aws directconnect create-private-virtual-interface --connection-id dxcon-fg31dyv6 --new-
    private-virtual-interface virtualInterfaceName=PrivateVirtualInterface,vlan=101,asn
    =65000,virtualGatewayId=vgw-ebaa27db,addressFamily=ipv4
```

```
1 {
2      "virtualInterfaceState": "pending",
3      "asn": 65000,
4      "vlan": 101,
5      "customerAddress": "192.168.1.2/30",
6      "ownerAccount": "123456789012",
7      "connectionId": "dxcon-fg31dyv6",
8      "addressFamily": "ipv4",
9      "virtualGatewayId": "vgw-ebaa27db",
10     "virtualInterfaceId": "dxvif-ffhhk74f",
11     "authKey": "asdf34example",
12     "routeFilterPrefixes": [],
13     "location": "TIVIT",
14     "bgpPeers": [
15         {
16             "bgpStatus": "down",
17             "customerAddress": "192.168.1.2/30",
18             "addressFamily": "ipv4",
19             "authKey": "asdf34example",
20             "bgpPeerState": "pending",
21             "amazonAddress": "192.168.1.1/30",
22             "asn": 65000
23         }
24     "customerRouterConfig": "<?xml version=\"1.0\" encoding=\"UTF-8\"?>\n<
        logical_connection id=\"dxvif-ffhhk74f\">\n  <vlan>101</vlan>\n  <customer_address
        >192.168.1.2/30</customer_address>\n  <amazon_address>192.168.1.1/30</
        amazon_address>\n  <bgp_asn>65000</bgp_asn>\n  <bgp_auth_key>asdf34example</
        bgp_auth_key>\n  <amazon_bgp_asn>7224</amazon_bgp_asn>\n  <connection_type>private
        </connection_type>\n</logical_connection>\n",
25     "amazonAddress": "192.168.1.1/30",
26     "virtualInterfaceType": "private",
27     "virtualInterfaceName": "PrivateVirtualInterface"
28 }
```

To create a private virtual interface that supports IPv6 traffic, use the same command as above and specify **ipv6** for the **addressFamily** parameter. You cannot specify your own IPv6 addresses for the BGP peering session; Amazon allocates you IPv6 addresses.

3. To view the router configuration information in XML format, describe the virtual interface you created. Use the `--query` parameter to extract the `customerRouterConfig` information, and the `--output` parameter to organize the text into tab-delimited lines.

```
aws directconnect describe-virtual-interfaces --virtual-interface-id dxvif-ffhhk74f --query
    virtualInterfaces[*].customerRouterConfig --output text
```

```xml
<?xml version="1.0" encoding="UTF-8"?>
<logical_connection id="dxvif-ffhhk74f">
  <vlan>101</vlan>
  <customer_address>192.168.1.2/30</customer_address>
  <amazon_address>192.168.1.1/30</amazon_address>
  <bgp_asn>65000</bgp_asn>
  <bgp_auth_key>asdf34example</bgp_auth_key>
  <amazon_bgp_asn>7224</amazon_bgp_asn>
  <connection_type>private</connection_type>
</logical_connection>
```

To create a public virtual interface

1. To create a public virtual interface, you must specify a name, a VLAN ID, and a BGP Autonomous System Number (ASN).

   For IPv4 traffic, you must also specify public IPv4 addresses for each end of the BGP peering session, and public IPv4 routes that you will advertise over BGP. The following example creates a public virtual interface for IPv4 traffic.

```
aws directconnect create-public-virtual-interface --connection-id dxcon-fg31dyv6 --new-
    public-virtual-interface virtualInterfaceName=PublicVirtualInterface,vlan=2000,asn
    =65000,amazonAddress=203.0.113.1/30,customerAddress=203.0.113.2/30,addressFamily=ipv4,
    routeFilterPrefixes=[{cidr=203.0.113.0/30},{cidr=203.0.113.4/30}]
```

```json
{
    "virtualInterfaceState": "verifying",
    "asn": 65000,
    "vlan": 2000,
    "customerAddress": "203.0.113.2/30",
    "ownerAccount": "123456789012",
    "connectionId": "dxcon-fg31dyv6",
    "addressFamily": "ipv4",
    "virtualGatewayId": "",
    "virtualInterfaceId": "dxvif-fgh0hcrk",
    "authKey": "asdf34example",
    "routeFilterPrefixes": [
        {
            "cidr": "203.0.113.0/30"
        },
        {
            "cidr": "203.0.113.4/30"
        }
    ],
    "location": "TIVIT",
    "bgpPeers": [
        {
            "bgpStatus": "down",
            "customerAddress": "203.0.113.2/30",
            "addressFamily": "ipv4",
```

```
26          "authKey": "asdf34example",
27          "bgpPeerState": "verifying",
28          "amazonAddress": "203.0.113.1/30",
29          "asn": 65000
30       }
31     ],
32     "customerRouterConfig": "<?xml version=\"1.0\" encoding=\"UTF-8\"?>\n<
          logical_connection id=\"dxvif-fgh0hcrk\">\n  <vlan>2000</vlan>\n  <customer_address
          >203.0.113.2/30</customer_address>\n  <amazon_address>203.0.113.1/30</
          amazon_address>\n  <bgp_asn>65000</bgp_asn>\n  <bgp_auth_key>asdf34example</
          bgp_auth_key>\n  <amazon_bgp_asn>7224</amazon_bgp_asn>\n  <connection_type>public</
          connection_type>\n</logical_connection>\n",
33     "amazonAddress": "203.0.113.1/30",
34     "virtualInterfaceType": "public",
35     "virtualInterfaceName": "PublicVirtualInterface"
36 }
```

To create a public virtual interface that supports IPv6 traffic, you can specify IPv6 routes that you will advertise over BGP. You cannot specify IPv6 addresses for the peering session; Amazon allocates IPv6 addresses to you. The following example creates a public virtual interface for IPv6 traffic.

```
1 aws directconnect create-public-virtual-interface --connection-id dxcon-fg31dyv6 --new-
    public-virtual-interface virtualInterfaceName=PublicVirtualInterface,vlan=2000,asn
    =65000,addressFamily=ipv6,routeFilterPrefixes=[{cidr=2001:db8:64ce:ba00::/64},{cidr
    =2001:db8:64ce:ba01::/64}]
```

2. To view the router configuration information in XML format, describe the virtual interface you created. Use the --query parameter to extract the customerRouterConfig information, and the --output parameter to organize the text into tab-delimited lines.

```
1 aws directconnect describe-virtual-interfaces --virtual-interface-id dxvif-fgh0hcrk --query
    virtualInterfaces[*].customerRouterConfig --output text
```

```
1 <?xml version="1.0" encoding="UTF-8"?>
2 <logical_connection id="dxvif-fgh0hcrk">
3   <vlan>2000</vlan>
4   <customer_address>203.0.113.2/30</customer_address>
5   <amazon_address>203.0.113.1/30</amazon_address>
6   <bgp_asn>65000</bgp_asn>
7   <bgp_auth_key>asdf34example</bgp_auth_key>
8   <amazon_bgp_asn>7224</amazon_bgp_asn>
9   <connection_type>public</connection_type>
10 </logical_connection>
```

Logging AWS Direct Connect API Calls in AWS CloudTrail

AWS Direct Connect is integrated with AWS CloudTrail, a service that captures API calls made by or on behalf of your AWS account. This information is collected and written to log files that are stored in an Amazon Simple Storage Service (S3) bucket that you specify. API calls are logged when you use the AWS Direct Connect API, the AWS Direct Connect console, a back-end console, or the AWS CLI. Using the information collected by CloudTrail, you can determine what request was made to AWS Direct Connect, the source IP address the request was made from, who made the request, when it was made, and so on.

To learn more about CloudTrail, including how to configure and enable it, see the AWS CloudTrail User Guide.

Topics

- AWS Direct Connect Information in CloudTrail
- Understanding AWS Direct Connect Log File Entries

AWS Direct Connect Information in CloudTrail

If CloudTrail logging is turned on, calls made to all AWS Direct Connect actions are captured in log files. All of the AWS Direct Connect actions are documented in the AWS Direct Connect API Reference. For example, calls to the **CreateConnection**, **CreatePrivateVirtualInterface**, and **DescribeConnections** actions generate entries in CloudTrail log files.

Every log entry contains information about who generated the request. For example, if a request is made to create a new connection to AWS Direct Connect (**CreateConnection**), CloudTrail logs the user identity of the person or service that made the request. The user identity information helps you determine whether the request was made with root credentials or AWS Identity and Access Management (IAM) user credentials, with temporary security credentials for a role or federated user, or by another service in AWS. For more information about CloudTrail fields, see CloudTrail Event Reference in the AWS CloudTrail User Guide.

You can store your log files in your bucket for as long as you want, but you can also define Amazon S3 lifecycle rules to archive or delete log files automatically. By default, your log files are encrypted by using Amazon S3 server-side encryption (SSE).

Understanding AWS Direct Connect Log File Entries

CloudTrail log files can contain one or more log entries composed of multiple JSON-formatted events. A log entry represents a single request from any source and includes information about the requested action, any input parameters, the date and time of the action, and so on. The log entries do not appear in any particular order. That is, they do not represent an ordered stack trace of the public API calls.

The following log file record shows that a user called the **CreateConnection** action.

```
1  {
2      "Records": [{
3          "eventVersion": "1.0",
4          "userIdentity": {
5              "type": "IAMUser",
6              "principalId": "EX_PRINCIPAL_ID",
7              "arn": "arn:aws:iam::123456789012:user/Alice",
8              "accountId": "123456789012",
9              "accessKeyId": "EXAMPLE_KEY_ID",
10             "userName": "Alice",
11             "sessionContext": {
12                 "attributes": {
13                     "mfaAuthenticated": "false",
```

```
14            "creationDate": "2014-04-04T12:23:05Z"
15           }
16         }
17      },
18      "eventTime": "2014-04-04T17:28:16Z",
19      "eventSource": "directconnect.amazonaws.com",
20      "eventName": "CreateConnection",
21      "awsRegion": "us-west-2",
22      "sourceIPAddress": "127.0.0.1",
23      "userAgent": "Coral/Jakarta",
24      "requestParameters": {
25         "location": "EqSE2",
26         "connectionName": "MyExampleConnection",
27         "bandwidth": "1Gbps"
28      },
29      "responseElements": {
30         "location": "EqSE2",
31         "region": "us-west-2",
32         "connectionState": "requested",
33         "bandwidth": "1Gbps",
34         "ownerAccount": "123456789012",
35         "connectionId": "dxcon-fhajolyy",
36         "connectionName": "MyExampleConnection"
37      }
38   },
39   ...additional entries
40   ]
41 }
```

The following log file record shows that a user called the **CreatePrivateVirtualInterface** action.

```
1 {
2    "Records": [
3    {
4       "eventVersion": "1.0",
5       "userIdentity": {
6          "type": "IAMUser",
7          "principalId": "EX_PRINCIPAL_ID",
8          "arn": "arn:aws:iam::123456789012:user/Alice",
9          "accountId": "123456789012",
10         "accessKeyId": "EXAMPLE_KEY_ID",
11         "userName": "Alice",
12         "sessionContext": {
13            "attributes": {
14               "mfaAuthenticated": "false",
15               "creationDate": "2014-04-04T12:23:05Z"
16            }
17         }
18      },
19      "eventTime": "2014-04-04T17:39:55Z",
20      "eventSource": "directconnect.amazonaws.com",
21      "eventName": "CreatePrivateVirtualInterface",
22      "awsRegion": "us-west-2",
23      "sourceIPAddress": "127.0.0.1",
24      "userAgent": "Coral/Jakarta",
```

```
25      "requestParameters": {
26          "connectionId": "dxcon-fhajolyy",
27          "newPrivateVirtualInterface": {
28              "virtualInterfaceName": "MyVirtualInterface",
29              "customerAddress": "[PROTECTED]",
30              "authKey": "[PROTECTED]",
31              "asn": -1,
32              "virtualGatewayId": "vgw-bb09d4a5",
33              "amazonAddress": "[PROTECTED]",
34              "vlan": 123
35          }
36      },
37      "responseElements": {
38          "virtualInterfaceId": "dxvif-fgq61m6w",
39          "authKey": "[PROTECTED]",
40          "virtualGatewayId": "vgw-bb09d4a5",
41          "customerRouterConfig": "[PROTECTED]",
42          "virtualInterfaceType": "private",
43          "asn": -1,
44          "routeFilterPrefixes": [],
45          "virtualInterfaceName": "MyVirtualInterface",
46          "virtualInterfaceState": "pending",
47          "customerAddress": "[PROTECTED]",
48          "vlan": 123,
49          "ownerAccount": "123456789012",
50          "amazonAddress": "[PROTECTED]",
51          "connectionId": "dxcon-fhajolyy",
52          "location": "EqSE2"
53      }
54  },
55  ...additional entries
56  ]
57 }
```

The following log file record shows that a user called the **DescribeConnections** action.

```
1 {
2    "Records": [
3    {
4        "eventVersion": "1.0",
5        "userIdentity": {
6            "type": "IAMUser",
7            "principalId": "EX_PRINCIPAL_ID",
8            "arn": "arn:aws:iam::123456789012:user/Alice",
9            "accountId": "123456789012",
10           "accessKeyId": "EXAMPLE_KEY_ID",
11           "userName": "Alice",
12           "sessionContext": {
13               "attributes": {
14                   "mfaAuthenticated": "false",
15                   "creationDate": "2014-04-04T12:23:05Z"
16               }
17           }
18       },
19       "eventTime": "2014-04-04T17:27:28Z",
```

```
20        "eventSource": "directconnect.amazonaws.com",
21        "eventName": "DescribeConnections",
22        "awsRegion": "us-west-2",
23        "sourceIPAddress": "127.0.0.1",
24        "userAgent": "Coral/Jakarta",
25        "requestParameters": null,
26        "responseElements": null
27     },
28     ...additional entries
29   ]
30 }
```

The following log file record shows that a user called the **DescribeVirtualInterfaces** action.

```
1  {
2      "Records": [
3          {
4              "eventVersion": "1.0",
5              "userIdentity": {
6                  "type": "IAMUser",
7                  "principalId": "EX_PRINCIPAL_ID",
8                  "arn": "arn:aws:iam::123456789012:user/Alice",
9                  "accountId": "123456789012",
10                 "accessKeyId": "EXAMPLE_KEY_ID",
11                 "userName": "Alice",
12                 "sessionContext": {
13                     "attributes": {
14                         "mfaAuthenticated": "false",
15                         "creationDate": "2014-04-04T12:23:05Z"
16                     }
17                 }
18             },
19             "eventTime": "2014-04-04T17:37:53Z",
20             "eventSource": "directconnect.amazonaws.com",
21             "eventName": "DescribeVirtualInterfaces",
22             "awsRegion": "us-west-2",
23             "sourceIPAddress": "127.0.0.1",
24             "userAgent": "Coral/Jakarta",
25             "requestParameters": {
26                 "connectionId": "dxcon-fhajolyy"
27             },
28             "responseElements": null
29         },
30         ...additional entries
31     ]
32 }
```

Monitoring AWS Direct Connect

Monitoring is an important part of maintaining the reliability, availability, and performance of your AWS Direct Connect resources. You should collect monitoring data from all of the parts of your AWS solution so that you can more easily debug a multi-point failure if one occurs. Before you start monitoring AWS Direct Connect; however, you should create a monitoring plan that includes answers to the following questions:

- What are your monitoring goals?
- What resources will you monitor?
- How often will you monitor these resources?
- What monitoring tools will you use?
- Who will perform the monitoring tasks?
- Who should be notified when something goes wrong?

The next step is to establish a baseline for normal AWS Direct Connect performance in your environment, by measuring performance at various times and under different load conditions. As you monitor AWS Direct Connect, store historical monitoring data so that you can compare it with current performance data, identify normal performance patterns and performance anomalies, and devise methods to address issues.

To establish a baseline, you should monitor the usage, state, and health of your physical AWS Direct Connect connections.

Topics

- Monitoring Tools
- Monitoring with Amazon CloudWatch

Monitoring Tools

AWS provides various tools that you can use to monitor an AWS Direct Connect connection. You can configure some of these tools to do the monitoring for you, while some of the tools require manual intervention. We recommend that you automate monitoring tasks as much as possible.

Automated Monitoring Tools

You can use the following automated monitoring tools to watch AWS Direct Connect and report when something is wrong:

- **Amazon CloudWatch Alarms** – Watch a single metric over a time period that you specify, and perform one or more actions based on the value of the metric relative to a given threshold over a number of time periods. The action is a notification sent to an Amazon SNS topic. CloudWatch alarms do not invoke actions simply because they are in a particular state; the state must have changed and been maintained for a specified number of periods. For more information, see Monitoring with Amazon CloudWatch.
- **AWS CloudTrail Log Monitoring** – Share log files between accounts, monitor CloudTrail log files in real time by sending them to CloudWatch Logs, write log processing applications in Java, and validate that your log files have not changed after delivery by CloudTrail. For more information, see Logging AWS Direct Connect API Calls in AWS CloudTrail and Working with CloudTrail Log Files in the *AWS CloudTrail User Guide*.

Manual Monitoring Tools

Another important part of monitoring an AWS Direct Connect connection involves manually monitoring those items that the CloudWatch alarms don't cover. The AWS Direct Connect and CloudWatch console dashboards provide an at-a-glance view of the state of your AWS environment.

- The AWS Direct Connect console shows:

  - Connection status (see the **State** column)
  - Virtual interface status (see the **State** column)

- The CloudWatch home page shows:

  - Current alarms and status
  - Graphs of alarms and resources
  - Service health status

  In addition, you can use CloudWatch to do the following:

  - Create customized dashboards to monitor the services you care about
  - Graph metric data to troubleshoot issues and discover trends
  - Search and browse all your AWS resource metrics
  - Create and edit alarms to be notified of problems

Monitoring with Amazon CloudWatch

You can monitor physical AWS Direct Connect connections using CloudWatch, which collects and processes raw data from AWS Direct Connect into readable, near real-time metrics. By default, CloudWatch provides AWS Direct Connect metric data in 5-minute intervals. You can optionally view data in 1-minute intervals.

For more information about Amazon CloudWatch, see the *Amazon CloudWatch User Guide*.

Note
If your connection is a hosted connection from an AWS Direct Connect partner, you cannot view CloudWatch metrics for the hosted connection.

Topics
- AWS Direct Connect Metrics and Dimensions
- Creating CloudWatch Alarms to Monitor AWS Direct Connect Connections

AWS Direct Connect Metrics and Dimensions

AWS Direct Connect sends the following metrics about your AWS Direct Connect connections at 30-second intervals to Amazon CloudWatch. Amazon CloudWatch then aggregates these data points to 1-minute or 5-minute intervals. You can use the following procedures to view the metrics for AWS Direct Connect connections.

To view metrics using the CloudWatch console

Metrics are grouped first by the service namespace, and then by the various dimension combinations within each namespace.

1. Open the CloudWatch console at https://console.aws.amazon.com/cloudwatch/.

2. In the navigation pane, choose **Metrics**.

3. Under **All metrics**, choose the **DX** metric namespace.

4. Choose **Connection Metrics**, and select the metric dimension to view the metrics (for example, for the AWS Direct Connect connection).

5. (Optional) To return data for the selected metric in 1-minute intervals, choose **Graphed metrics**, and select **1 Minute** from the **Period** list.

To view metrics using the AWS Direct Connect console

1. Open the AWS Direct Connect console at https://console.aws.amazon.com/directconnect/.

2. In the navigation pane, choose **Connections** and select your connection.

3. The **Monitoring** tab displays the metrics for your connection.

To view metrics using the AWS CLI

- At a command prompt, use the following command:

```
1 aws cloudwatch list-metrics --namespace "AWS/DX"
```

The following metrics are available from AWS Direct Connect. Metrics are currently available for AWS Direct Connect physical connections only.

Metric	Description
ConnectionState	The state of the connection. 0 indicates DOWN and 1 indicates UP. Units: Boolean

Metric	Description
ConnectionBpsEgress	The bit rate for outbound data from the AWS side of the connection. The number reported is the aggregate over the specified time period (5 minutes by default, 1 minute minimum). Units: Bits per second
ConnectionBpsIngress	The bit rate for inbound data to the AWS side of the connection. The number reported is the aggregate over the specified time period (5 minutes by default, 1 minute minimum). Units: Bits per second
ConnectionPpsEgress	The packet rate for outbound data from the AWS side of the connection. The number reported is the aggregate over the specified time period (5 minutes by default, 1 minute minimum). Units: Packets per second
ConnectionPpsIngress	The packet rate for inbound data to the AWS side of the connection. The number reported is the aggregate over the specified time period (5 minutes by default, 1 minute minimum). Units: Packets per second
ConnectionCRCErrorCount	The number of times cyclic redundancy check (CRC) errors are observed for the data received at the connection. Units: Integer
ConnectionLightLevelTx	Indicates the health of the fiber connection for egress (outbound) traffic from the AWS side of the connection. This metric is available for connections with 10 Gbps port speeds only. Units: dBm
ConnectionLightLevelRx	Indicates the health of the fiber connection for ingress (inbound) traffic to the AWS side of the connection. This metric is available for connections with 10 Gbps port speeds only. Units: dBm

You can filter the AWS Direct Connect data using the following dimensions.

Dimension	Description
ConnectionId	This dimension filters the data by the AWS Direct Connect connection.

Creating CloudWatch Alarms to Monitor AWS Direct Connect Connections

You can create a CloudWatch alarm that sends an Amazon SNS message when the alarm changes state. An alarm watches a single metric over a time period that you specify, and sends a notification to an Amazon SNS topic based on the value of the metric relative to a given threshold over a number of time periods.

For example, you can create an alarm that monitors the state of an AWS Direct Connect connection and sends a notification when the connection state is DOWN for 5 consecutive 1-minute periods.

To create an alarm for connection state

1. Open the CloudWatch console at https://console.aws.amazon.com/cloudwatch/.

2. In the navigation pane, choose **Alarms**, **Create Alarm**.

3. Choose the **DX Metrics** category.

4. Select the AWS Direct Connect connection and choose the **ConnectionState** metric. Choose **Next**.

5. Configure the alarm as follows, and choose **Create Alarm** when you are done:

   - Under **Alarm Threshold**, enter a name and description for your alarm. For **Whenever**, choose $<$ and enter 1. Enter **5** for the consecutive periods.
   - Under **Actions**, select an existing notification list or choose **New list** to create a new one.
   - Under **Alarm Preview**, select a period of 1 minute.

For more examples of creating alarms, see Creating Amazon CloudWatch Alarms in the *Amazon CloudWatch User Guide*.

Troubleshooting AWS Direct Connect

The following topics can help you troubleshoot issues with your AWS Direct Connect connection.

Topics

- Troubleshooting Layer 1 (Physical) Issues
- Troubleshooting Layer 2 (Data Link) Issues
- Troubleshooting Layer 3/4 (Network/Transport) Issues
- Troubleshooting Routing Issues

Troubleshooting Layer 1 (Physical) Issues

If you or your network provider are having difficulty establishing physical connectivity to an AWS Direct Connect device, use the following steps to troubleshoot the issue.

1. Verify with the colocation provider that the cross connect is complete. Ask them or your network provider to provide you with a cross connect completion notice and compare the ports with those listed on your LOA-CFA.

2. Verify that your router or your provider's router is powered on and that the ports are activated.

3. Ensure that the routers are using the correct optical transceiver, auto-negotiation is disabled, and port speed and full-duplex mode are manually configured. For more information, see Network Requirements.

4. Verify that the router is receiving an acceptable optical signal over the cross connect.

5. Try flipping (also known as rolling) the Tx/Rx fiber strands.

6. Check the Amazon CloudWatch metrics for AWS Direct Connect. You can verify the AWS Direct Connect device's Tx/Rx optical readings (10-Gbps port speeds only), physical error count, and operational status. For more information, see Monitoring with Amazon CloudWatch.

7. Contact the colocation provider and request a written report for the Tx/Rx optical signal across the cross connect.

8. If the above steps do not resolve physical connectivity issues, contact AWS Support and provide the cross connect completion notice and optical signal report from the colocation provider.

The following flow chart contains the steps to diagnose issues with the physical connection.

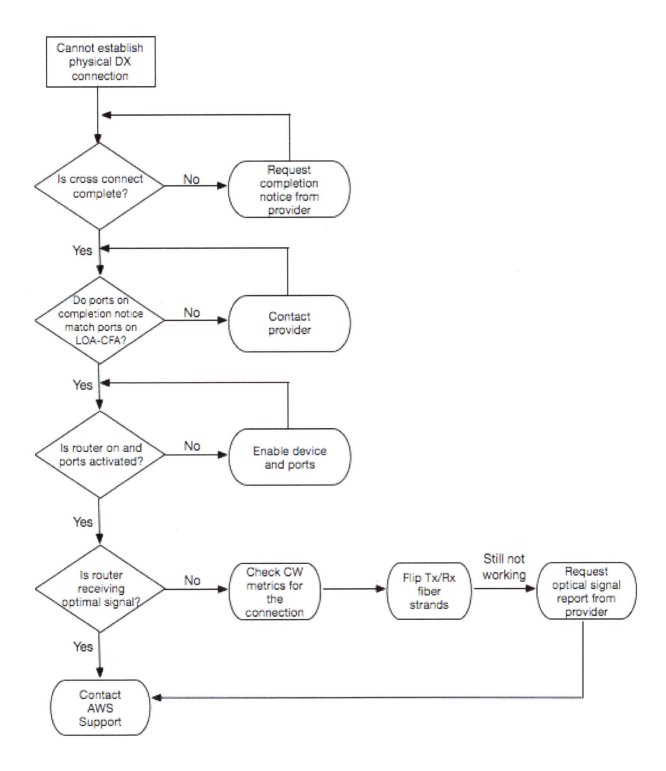

Troubleshooting Layer 2 (Data Link) Issues

If your AWS Direct Connect physical connection is up but your virtual interface is down, use the following steps to troubleshoot the issue.

1. If you cannot ping the Amazon peer IP address, verify that your peer IP address is configured correctly and in the correct VLAN. Ensure that the IP address is configured in the VLAN subinterface and not the physical interface (for example, GigabitEthernet0/0.123 instead of GigabitEthernet0/0).

2. Verify if the router has a MAC address entry from the AWS endpoint in your address resolution protocol (ARP) table.

3. Ensure that any intermediate devices between endpoints have VLAN trunking enabled for your 802.1Q VLAN tag. ARP cannot be established on the AWS side until AWS receives tagged traffic.

4. Clear your or your provider's ARP table cache.

5. If the above steps do not establish ARP or you still cannot ping the Amazon peer IP, contact AWS Support.

The following flow chart contains the steps to diagnose issues with the data link.

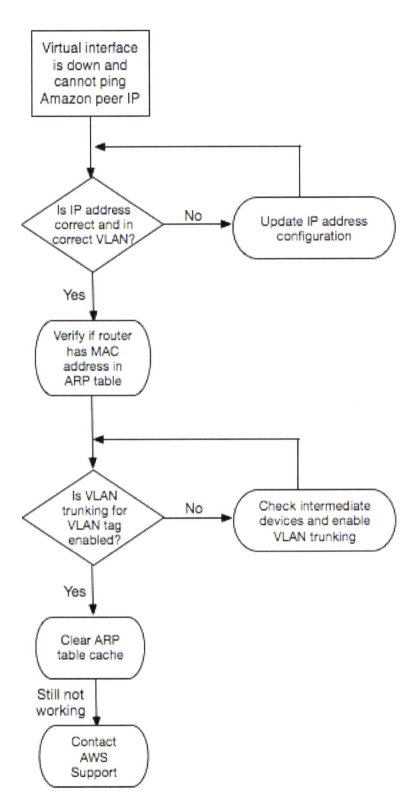

If the BGP session is still not established after verifying these steps, see Troubleshooting Layer 3/4 (Network/-Transport) Issues. If the BGP session is established but you are experiencing routing issues, see Troubleshooting Routing Issues.

Troubleshooting Layer 3/4 (Network/Transport) Issues

If your AWS Direct Connect physical connection is up and you can ping the Amazon peer IP address, but your virtual interface is down and the BGP peering session cannot be established, use the following steps to troubleshoot the issue.

1. Ensure that your BGP local Autonomous System Number (ASN) and Amazon's ASN are configured correctly.

2. Ensure that the peer IPs for both sides of the BGP peering session are configured correctly.

3. Ensure that your MD5 authentication key is configured and exactly matches the key in the downloaded router configuration file. Check that there are no extra spaces or characters.

4. Verify that you or your provider are not advertising more than 100 prefixes for private virtual interfaces or 1,000 prefixes for public virtual interfaces. These are hard limits and cannot be exceeded.

5. Ensure that there are no firewall or ACL rules that are blocking TCP port 179 or any high-numbered ephemeral TCP ports. These ports are necessary for BGP to establish a TCP connection between the peers.

6. Check your BGP logs for any errors or warning messages.

7. If the above steps do not establish the BGP peering session, contact AWS Support.

The following flow chart contains the steps to diagnose issues with the BGP peering session.

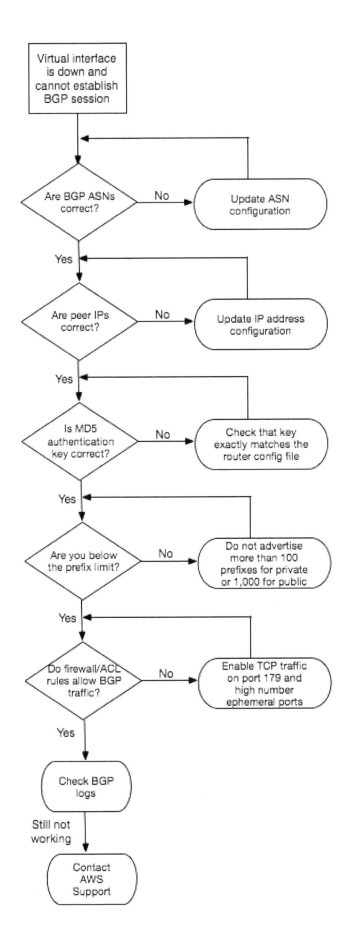

If the BGP peering session is established but you are experiencing routing issues, see Troubleshooting Routing Issues.

Troubleshooting Routing Issues

If your virtual interface is up and you've established a BGP peering session but you cannot route traffic over the virtual interface, use the following steps to troubleshoot the issue.

1. Ensure that you are advertising a route for your on-premises network prefix over the BGP session. For a private virtual interface, this can be a private or public network prefix. For a public virtual interface, this must be your publicly routable network prefix.

2. For a private virtual interface, ensure that your VPC security groups and network ACLs allow inbound and outbound traffic for your on-premises network prefix. For more information, see Security Groups and Network ACLs in the *Amazon VPC User Guide*.

3. For a private virtual interface, ensure that your VPC route tables have prefixes pointing to the virtual private gateway to which your private virtual interface is connected. For example, if you prefer to have all your traffic routed towards your on-premises network by default, you can add the default route (0.0.0.0/0 and/or ::/0) with the virtual private gateway as the target in your VPC route tables.

   - Alternatively, enable route propagation to automatically update routes in your route tables based on your dynamic BGP route advertisement. You can have up to 100 propagated routes per route table. This limit cannot be increased. For more information, see Enabling and Disabling Route Propagation in the *Amazon VPC User Guide*.

4. If the above steps do not resolve your routing issues, contact AWS Support.

The following flow chart contains the steps to diagnose routing issues.

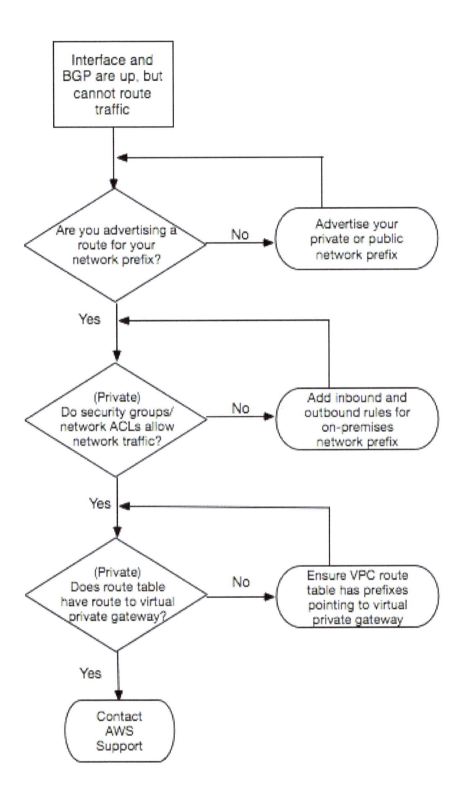

Document History

- **API version:** 2012-10-25

The following table describes the important changes since the last release of the *AWS Direct Connect User Guide*.

Change	Description	Release Date
Local preference BGP communities	You can use local preference BGP community tags to achieve load balancing and route preference for incoming traffic to your network. For more information, see Local Preference BGP Communities.	2018-02-06
AWS Direct Connect gateway	You can use a Direct Connect gateway to connect your AWS Direct Connect connection to VPCs in remote regions. For more information, see Direct Connect Gateways.	2017-11-01
Amazon CloudWatch metrics	You can view CloudWatch metrics for your AWS Direct Connect connections. For more information, see Monitoring with Amazon CloudWatch.	2017-06-29
Link aggregation groups	You can create a link aggregation group (LAG) to aggregate multiple AWS Direct Connect connections. For more information, see Link Aggregation Groups.	2017-02-13
IPv6 support	Your virtual interface can now support an IPv6 BGP peering session. For more information, see Adding or Removing a BGP Peer.	2016-12-01
Tagging support	You can now tag your AWS Direct Connect resources. For more information, see Using Tags with AWS Direct Connect.	2016-11-04
Self-service LOA-CFA	You can now download your Letter of Authorization and Connecting Facility Assignment (LOA-CFA) using the AWS Direct Connect console or API.	2016-06-22
New location in Silicon Valley	Updated topic to include the addition of the new Silicon Valley location in the US West (N. California) region.	2016-06-03

Change	Description	Release Date
New location in Amsterdam	Updated topic to include the addition of the new Amsterdam location in the EU (Frankfurt) region.	2016-05-19
New locations in Portland, Oregon and Singapore	Updated topic to include the addition of the new Portland, Oregon and Singapore locations in the US West (Oregon) and Asia Pacific (Singapore) regions.	2016-04-27
New location in Sao Paulo, Brasil	Updated topic to include the addition of the new Sao Paulo location in the South America (São Paulo) region.	2015-12-09
New locations in Dallas, London, Silicon Valley, and Mumbai	Updated topics to include the addition of the new locations in Dallas (US East (N. Virginia) region), London (EU (Ireland) region), Silicon Valley (AWS GovCloud (US) region), and Mumbai (Asia Pacific (Singapore) region).	2015-11-27
New location in the China (Beijing) region	Updated topics to include the addition of the new Beijing location in the China (Beijing) region.	2015-04-14
New Las Vegas location in the US West (Oregon) region	Updated topics to include the addition of the new AWS Direct Connect Las Vegas location in the US West (Oregon) region.	2014-11-10
New EU (Frankfurt) region	Updated topics to include the addition of the new AWS Direct Connect locations serving the EU (Frankfurt) region.	2014-10-23
New locations in the Asia Pacific (Sydney) region	Updated topics to include the addition of the new AWS Direct Connect locations serving the Asia Pacific (Sydney) region.	2014-07-14
Support for AWS CloudTrail	Added a new topic to explain how you can use CloudTrail to log activity in AWS Direct Connect. For more information, see Logging AWS Direct Connect API Calls in AWS CloudTrail.	2014-04-04
Support for accessing remote AWS regions	Added a new topic to explain how you can access public resources in a remote region. For more information, see Accessing a Remote AWS Region.	2013-12-19

Change	Description	Release Date
Support for hosted connections	Updated topics to include support for hosted connections.	2013-10-22
New location in the EU (Ireland) region	Updated topics to include the addition of the new AWS Direct Connect location serving the EU (Ireland) region.	2013-06-24
New Seattle location in the US West (Oregon) region	Updated topics to include the addition of the new AWS Direct Connect location in Seattle serving the US West (Oregon) region.	2013-05-08
Support for using IAM with AWS Direct Connect	Added a topic about using AWS Identity and Access Management with AWS Direct Connect. For more information, see Using AWS Identity and Access Management with AWS Direct Connect.	2012-12-21
New Asia Pacific (Sydney) region	Updated topics to include the addition of the new AWS Direct Connect location serving the Asia Pacific (Sydney) region.	2012-12-14
New AWS Direct Connect console, and the US East (N. Virginia) and South America (Sao Paulo) regions	Replaced the AWS Direct Connect Getting Started Guide with the AWS Direct Connect User Guide. Added new topics to cover the new AWS Direct Connect console, added a billing topic, added router configuration information, and updated topics to include the addition of two new AWS Direct Connect locations serving the US East (N. Virginia) and South America (Sao Paulo) regions.	2012-08-13
Support for the EU (Ireland), Asia Pacific (Singapore), and Asia Pacific (Tokyo) regions	Added a new troubleshooting section and updated topics to include the addition of four new AWS Direct Connect locations serving the US West (Northern California), EU (Ireland), Asia Pacific (Singapore), and Asia Pacific (Tokyo) regions.	2012-01-10
Support for the US West (Northern California) region	Updated topics to include the addition of the US West (Northern California) region.	2011-09-08
Public release	The first release of AWS Direct Connect.	2011-08-03

AWS Glossary

For the latest AWS terminology, see the AWS Glossary in the *AWS General Reference*.

www.ingramcontent.com/pod-product-compliance
Lightning Source LLC
LaVergne TN
LVHW082040050326
832904LV00005B/256